# The Digital Teaching Portfolio Handbook

## A HOW-TO GUIDE FOR EDUCATORS

**CLARE R. KILBANE**
*University of Massachusetts at Amherst*

**NATALIE B. MILMAN**
*The George Washington University*

I0609666

Boston I New York I San Francisco
Mexico City I Montreal I Toronto I London I Madrid I Munich I Paris
Hong Kong I Singapore I Tokyo I Cape Town I Sydney

**Executive Editor and Publisher:** *Stephen D. Dragin*
**Series Editorial Assistant:** *Barbara Strickland*
**Marketing Manager:** *Tara Whorf*
**Production Editor:** *Michael Granger*
**Editorial Production Service:** *Modern Graphics, Inc.*
**Composition Buyer:** *Linda Cox*
**Manufacturing Buyer:** *JoAnne Sweeney*
**Cover Administrator:** *Kristina Mose-Libon*
**Electronic Composition:** *Modern Graphics, Inc.*
**Text Design:** *Carol Somberg*

For related titles and support materials, visit our online catalog at www.ablongman.com.

Between the time Web site information is gathered and then published, it is not unusual for some sites to have closed. Also, the transcription of URLs can result in unintended typographical errors. The publisher would appreciate notification where these errors occur so that they may be corrected in subsequent editions.

**Library of Congress Cataloging-in-Publication Data**

Kilbane, Clare R.
    The digital teaching portfolio handbook : a how-to guide for educators / Clare R.
Kilbane, Natalie B. Milman.
      p. cm.
    Includes bibliographical references and index.
    ISBN 0-205-34345-7
      1. Portfolios in education—Computer-aided design—Handbooks, manuals, etc.
  2. Teachers—Rating of—Handbooks, manuals, etc.   I. Milman, Natalie B.   II. Title.

LB1029.P67 K52 2003
371.14′4—dc21

                                        2002071680

Printed in the United States of America

10  9  8  7  6  5  4  3  2  1     07  06  05  04  03  02

*To our parents who gave us life
and to Dennis, Doug, and Nadia who gave it new meaning.*

# contents

**v**

part two

THE DIGITAL TEACHING PORTFOLIO PROCESS   37

chapter **5**  Planning your Digital Teaching Portfolio   41

chapter **6**  Considering Digital Teaching Portfolio Materials   54

part three

## THINKING ABOUT PUTTING "DIGITAL" INTO YOUR TEACHING PORTFOLIO   93

## chapter 10   Things to Consider Before and After Getting Started   95

## chapter 11   Selecting a Design Tool   105

# ▌f i g u r e s ▌

# ▌t a b l e s ▌

# Digital Teaching Portfolios
# Build Better Teachers

My great, great-grandfather, Daniel William McGrath, was born in New York in 1854—the oldest son of Irish immigrants. He moved with his family to London, Ohio in 1856. There he received a grade-school education and worked on his father's farm. At the age of twenty, D.W, as he came to be called, left home for Columbus, Ohio, where he learned bricklaying. First he was a hired hand, then a journeyman, and later a foreman. In 1884, D.W. started his own business as a brick contractor—later branching out as a general contractor. In time, he was recognized as one of the most prolific contractors in Columbus, Ohio—building many of early Ohio's skyscrapers and bridges, as well as most of the main buildings on the original campus of the The Ohio State University (OSU).

Even though I grew up just minutes from the OSU campus, it was not until I started work on my Master's degree that I fully began to appreciate the legacy that had been left for me. On days when I managed to escape my classroom quickly after the last bell and get to campus with extra time before evening classes started, I toured D.W.'s buildings along the famed "oval" in the center of the OSU campus. It was fascinating to think that a first-generation American with only a basic education could have had a hand in creating such detailed and lasting edifices.

After a long day of teaching, my mind wandered as I walked past D.W's buildings on campus. I wondered whether D.W. would have found much use for the books in the William Oxley Thompson Memorial Library that he helped to build. I also could not help considering whether D.W could possibly have been as tired at the end of a day as I was. Surely directing bricklayers, masons, and framers was difficult, but could it be as exhausting as directing fourth-graders through reading, writing, and social studies!?

Eventually, I recognized that D.W. and I, despite the fact that we were different genders and were divided by nearly a 100 years of history, had many things in common. We shared a love for our chosen professions. That I knew to be true. But we also shared similar skills and challenges in our chosen professions. Both of us, contractor and teacher, worked in the public eye. We often were forced to take risks based on incomplete information and could be held accountable for the actions of others. As part of our daily work, we were required to implement carefully constructed plans, solve dynamic problems, effectively manage resources, and encourage different personalities to work together. Both of us had ended up in professions that required us to work incrementally toward goals that might take years to achieve!

Other days the differences in our work were more apparent than the similarities. For one, D.W. was well paid. He was also respected and recognized for his work. But the most visible difference in our daily jobs is quite clear to me when I look at D.W.'s legacies of brick, stone, and slate. As a teacher, the product of my daily labor is difficult to pinpoint and even harder to see. But most days, D.W. had tangible, physical evidence by which he could measure his accomplishments and communicate them with others. If only I could be so lucky!

Teachers, although they often stare at their students' work until they are blue in the face, rarely have the time or inclination to look with satisfaction upon their own. As a result, they often lack the affirmation resulting from the recognition of a job well done. However, there are methods for accumulating and communicating the evidence of teaching success. Teachers have within their power a way to recognize and celebrate their own achievements. They can do this through the creation of professional or teaching portfolios. These portfolios can compile the evidence of their professionalism and competence so that they can measure their own success. When published in digital or electronic format, portfolios carry a message of professionalism that can be easily shared with the local and global community and endure over time.

In this book, Natalie Milman and I present a plan for how teachers might use teaching portfolios to celebrate their professional growth and help others recognize their accomplishments. Like individual bricks in a building, the distinct, professional artifacts included in teaching portfolios such as lesson plans, course syllabi, photographs, and student evaluations can form something substantial and beautiful when arranged in deliberate, creative ways. Assembled in a portfolio, these materials demonstrate the accomplishments resulting from successful planning, effective problem solving, unleashed creativity, applied professional knowledge, relentless diligence, and unbridled enthusiasm. Professional portfolios are creations that communicate both excellence and artistry.

Because modern digital tools promise to revolutionize the creation of teaching portfolios as significantly as modern construction tools did the building process, we advocate their integration in all stages of the development of a teaching portfolio. High-tech tools offer many advantages. In addition to saving a teacher's time and energy, these tools, once teachers have mastered their use, can provide teachers greater freedom in the creative process. Teachers can benefit personally and professionally when using digital tools to facilitate the creation of teaching materials, the selection of professional artifacts, the organization of information, the packaging of professional work, and the sharing of materials in a portfolio with others.

This book is divided into three parts. Part one communicates ideas about portfolios in general and digital teaching portfolios in particular. It explores ways that the creation and use of digital teaching portfolios might positively influence teachers and others who work in the field of education. In Part two, we describe the steps involved in the process of creating a digital teaching portfolio. We present practical strategies for framing, organizing, assembling, producing, and evaluating a digital portfolio, as well as activities that will help teachers collect, select, and reflect on materials for inclusion in the portfolios. Part three presents information that should be considered before, during, and after creating a digital teaching portfolio—from tips for making the process easier to the types of hardware and software one might consider in designing a portfolio. In this part we also include a discussion of graphic design and ways to improve the visual presentation of a digital teaching portfolio. The appendices include additional information and resources that might be helpful, such as consent forms, and a special section on portfolios for school principals.

We hope that this book will be useful to teachers who work with students of all ages—from preschoolers to Ph.D.s. Although its primary audience is teacher candidates and inservice educators who work with children in K–12 learning environments, it also might be useful to those who work with these teachers and instructors who teach at colleges and universities. This book presents a comprehensive collection of information regarding the rationale and procedures for creating traditional portfolios in "hard-copy" format, and it builds on this foundation to suggest how new technological tools can transform the portfolio process and the product resulting from it.

—CRK

# part one

# The Case for Digital Teaching Portfolios

The first part of this book presents foundational information on portfolios and describes ways that the production of professional teaching portfolios might benefit educators and those associated with education. Chapter 1 defines the many different types of portfolios and suggests how digital tools may revolutionize both the portfolio-creation process as well as the finished product. Chapter 2 explores why teaching portfolios are growing in popularity and examines connections between larger societal trends and the portfolio movement. Chapters 3 and 4 communicate the benefits that teachers, principals, school districts, and schools of education may experience when creating and sharing teaching portfolios in various formats.

# chapter

# one

# 1

# Portfolios, Teaching Portfolios, and Digital Teaching Portfolios

pōrt-'fō-lē-ō (noun), plural, pōrt-'fō-lē-ōs

What comes to mind when you think of the word *portfolio*? Perhaps some of your first thoughts are similar to our own—it reminds us of the portfolios we had to create in our high school art classes. According to Merriam Webster's Collegiate Dictionary (http://merriamwebster.com), the word *portfolio* first appeared in 1722. It is derived from the Italian word *portafoglio*. The word is derived from *portare* (the Latin origin, *portar*, which means to carry) and *foglio*, which means leaf, sheet. *Merriam-Webster* (2002) defines a portfolio as,

1. a hinged cover or flexible case for carrying loose papers, pictures, or pamphlets,
2. the office and functions of a minister of state or member of a cabinet (from the use of such a case to carry documents of state) and
3. the securities held by an investor: the commercial paper held by a financial house (as a bank),

**3**

4. a set of pictures (as drawings or photographs) either bound in book form or loose in a folder.

Although these definitions differ from the accepted meaning of the word as it is used in the field of education, some connections exist. Portfolios, as educators know them, are often stored in flexible cases such as binders and folders. Their contents commonly demonstrate the functions of a person who to a classroom of children can be as important and powerful as a government dignitary. Inside a portfolio you'll find materials every bit as valuable and precious to teachers as securities are to investors!

In this chapter, we present information about the different types of portfolios that teachers create and explain their use in the field of education. We also describe some of the advantages and disadvantages of creating portfolios in digital format.

# Portfolios

A portfolio is a goal-driven, organized collection of artifacts that demonstrates a person's expansion of knowledge and skills over time. The contents, organization, and presentation of materials in portfolios vary greatly depending on their audience and purpose. However, all portfolios display tangible evidence of an individual's growth and development.

# Professional Portfolios

Professional portfolios can be described as purposeful compilations of and reflections on a professional's work, effort, and progress in their field. Portfolios are used in various professions, including architecture, the arts, and education. These portfolios, in their most basic form, are documentation tools that capture vivid "snapshots" of critical moments in a professional's growth. Portfolios illustrate these moments through various physical artifacts. For example, an artist's portfolio might display samples of art that demonstrate the ability to create using a variety of media—clay sculpture, watercolor painting, and wood-block printing. Written commentary from the artists, sharing their perception of their own work, might illustrate the artists' knowledge of techniques specific to each creative medium. A selection of "masterpieces" based on the artists' personal preferences enables them to showcase their talents over the course of their career.

There are essentially two types of professional portfolios: working portfolios and presentation portfolios. These types of portfolios differ based on their intended purpose and audience.

## Working Portfolios

Working portfolios are generally large, complete compilations of a person's work over a period of time. Working portfolios contain samples of a professionals' work from throughout their entire career, or they may encompass a shorter time period. For example, a teacher's portfolio might include lesson plans, units, photographs, software programs, multimedia presentations, and other teacher-created materials created over a school year or career. Working portfolios are stored in many different containers, including fancy leather notebooks, large canvas bags, boxes, milk crates, folders, computer hard drives, disks, or even CDs. Regardless of their size and shape, working portfolios serve as storage containers for a vast array of artifacts that demonstrate an individual's strengths and weaknesses, successes and failures, in their professional work. The working portfolio is often used in conjunction with a presentation portfolio. Table 1.1 outlines two types of working portfolios.

## Presentation Portfolios

Items in a presentation portfolio or "showcase portfolio" represent a subset of materials found in a professional's working portfolio. The materials might be selected as representative pieces from the working portfolio for a variety of reasons, but all are carefully chosen after reflection. Various criteria are used in selecting materials for inclusion in a presentation portfolio. For example, materials might be selected to reflect specific goals or a set of standards. In these instances, the portfolios might become *evaluative* portfolios. Professional groups in a variety of fields have developed standards that are being used as guidelines for the presentation of portfolios. In other instances, a portfolio might be created for a specific audience or a group of individuals. For example, an architect might create a portfolio to display competence in a particular area of work for a specific job they are seeking. Portfolios used for this purpose are often called *employment portfolios*. See Table 1.2 to learn about the different types of presentation portfolios one might encounter or choose to create.

### TABLE 1.1

### Types of Working Portfolios

| Portfolio Type | Purpose | Materials Usually Included |
|---|---|---|
| Descriptive (Campbell et al., 2000; Halaydna 1997; Shackelford 1997) | Foster reflection and self-assessment, focus on describing all the steps to learning | Detailed journal or work log |
| Learning | Foster reflection and self-assessment, emphasize an individual's work and learning in progress | Graphic organizers, outlines, working drafts that include notes and edited items, reflective statements about portfolio's components, professional development goals |

## TABLE 1.2

### Types of Presentation Portfolios

| Portfolio Type | Purpose | Materials Usually Included |
| --- | --- | --- |
| Assessment (a.k.a. Evaluative) (Wolf and Dietz 1998) | Present information about an individual's mastery of specific objectives and skills | Tests, competencies, and assignments based on specific predetermined criteria |
| Class (a.k.a. Composite) (Campbell et al. 2000; Halaydna 1997; Shackelford 1997) | Illustrate group (or class) efforts, progress, and accomplishments | Examples of student work, summary sheets for each student, description of expected student outcomes |
| Employment (Wolf and Dietz 1998) | Provide employers with information about a candidate | Resume, transcripts, letters of recommendation, awards, lesson plans |
| Showcase (Wolf and Dietz 1998) | To demonstrate an individual's best work, usually a collection of best-work samples | Completed works, final products |
| Teaching (Wolf and Dietz 1998) | Promotes teacher and student learning | Teacher and student work samples |

# Teaching Portfolios

A teaching portfolio is a special type of presentation portfolio that demonstrates the professional competence of anyone who engages in the act of teaching at any academic level. Although more widespread use of teaching portfolios occurs at the K–12 levels, teaching portfolios for college instructors are gaining popularity. Many institutions across the country are beginning to use these portfolios during the tenure and merit review processes. Traditionally, teaching portfolios contain a variety of materials or artifacts from teaching. These artifacts may include curricular units, syllabi, communication with students (e.g., e-mail, notes, etc.), writing samples, photographs, and videos. Professional documents such as letters of recommendation, records of academic course work, and teaching evaluations are also included. Although a teaching portfolio does teach those viewing it about the creator's professional competence, its name is derived from the type of work it displays rather than the instructional work it performs.

Teaching portfolios have several critical attributes. According to Lee Shulman (1998), President of the Carnegie Foundation for the Advancement of Teaching, a teaching portfolio is a "structured documentary history of a set of coached or mentored acts of teaching, substantiated by samples of student portfolios, and fully realized only through reflective writing, deliberation, and conversation" (p. 37). As Shulman suggests, the deliberate selection, reflection, and communication revolving around the materials included in a true teaching portfolio distinguish it from other types of portfolios that might be used to organize information for employment or other such purposes.

# Teaching Portfolio Trends

Teaching portfolios have been increasing in popularity since the early 1990s. Several reasons explain this trend. One reason is that various professional groups concerned with teacher quality have encouraged preservice and inservice teachers to create teaching portfolios. The National Board for Professional Teaching Standards (NBPTS) and the Interstate New Teachers Assessment Support Consortium (INTASC) promote teaching portfolios as an authentic means for demonstrating the many facets of a teacher's professionalism. These groups also consider portfolios the best method of illustrating an individual teacher's attainment of certain professional standards. See Chapter 2 for more information about professional organizations and standards.

Another reason for the growing popularity of teaching portfolios is that teachers benefit personally and professionally from the portfolio creation process. Many teachers discover that the learning process required to create a portfolio is a valuable opportunity to develop new knowledge and skills (i.e., those related to multimedia technology). Some find that the personal reflection required in selecting materials to include from past professional activities provides a much-needed exercise for measuring current competence and charting future professional growth. Many educators value their teaching portfolios as physical reminders of professional effort and growth that can be celebrated and shared with others. More of the benefits resulting from the creation of teaching portfolios are discussed in Chapter 3.

# Digital Teaching Portfolios

Digital teaching portfolios, sometimes referred to as multimedia portfolios, electronic portfolios, e-folios, webfolios, and electronically-augmented portfolios, contain much of the content traditional teaching portfolios include but present the materials in digital format. In digital teaching portfolios, professional materials, are presented using a combination of multimedia technologies, including, but not limited to, audio recordings; hypermedia programs; and database, spreadsheet, video, and word processing software. Such portfolios are stored on disks, CDs, Zip disks, or file servers accessible through the World Wide Web. In the future, if dreams of paperless offices and workplaces where most written communication occurs in digital format becomes a reality, it may not be necessary to call portfolios produced digitally "digital teaching portfolios." Until then, we will use this phrase to distinguish them from traditional portfolios that present "hard copies" of professional materials in binders or other containers.

Many experts recognize the advantages of digital teaching portfolios over their more traditional hard-copy counterpart. Lieberman and Rueter (1997) suggest, "[the] electronically enhanced portfolio augments the traditional print portfolio with electronic materials that can strengthen particular portfolio components" (p. 46). Although traditional portfolios presented in binders, notebooks, or other carrying cases are limited in how they display particular portfolio components, such as classroom teaching videos, high-tech instructional materials, software programs, and the like, multimedia portfolios can facilitate the viewing of these materials in a seamless, easy-to-use interface. Decisions regarding the methods used to publish a digital teaching portfolio are usually influenced by the teacher's technology experience, resources available, the goals of the portfolio, and the intended audience.

New hardware and software tools promise to revolutionize both the process and products associated with portfolios. The content included in a portfolio and the method of presenting this content change when technology is incorporated. The development and application of user-friendly software programs facilitates the portfolio development process by making it easier for teachers to organize and present material. The creation of new, more powerful multimedia authoring environments adds dimensions to the presentation of professional competence by enabling more engaging, sensory-rich displays (e.g., video clips). New distribution formats such as the World Wide Web and CD-ROM promote the sharing of portfolios among members of the educational community.

## Advantages of Digital Teaching Portfolios

Digital teaching portfolios offer several advantages over those produced on paper. Some relate to the presentation of digital teaching portfolios, such as increased accessibility and portability. Others relate to the production of digital teaching portfolios, such as enhanced creativity and increased teacher self-confidence. In the following sections, we elaborate on these in more detail.

**ACCESSIBILITY.**   Digital teaching portfolios offer certain advantages related to accessibility. Because digital resources can be reproduced easily and inexpensively, portfolios in digital format also can be reproduced easily and inexpensively. As a result, materials can be made available to a larger and wider audience. For example, when burned on CD, teaching portfolios can be distributed to an entire school community at low cost and without the need to make multiple copies of sometimes unwieldy teaching artifacts. Digital teaching portfolios also offer the advantage of being accessible from multiple locations and by many individuals simultaneously. When shared on the World Wide Web, portfolios displaying teachers' credentials are available at anytime, to anyone, in any location. And perhaps most useful, materials that might be needed in the classroom can be reproduced in digital format leaving the originals available to students in teachers' classrooms!

**PORTABILITY.**   Digital teaching portfolios are easier to transport than those produced in hard copy. This is another reason they can be shared more easily with large groups of people. Traditional portfolios, because they use the original materials created by teachers for use by students, often are large, bulky, and difficult to transport. Even though teachers often develop muscles from lugging heavy teachers' manuals around, they appreciate not having to use these muscles when they can share lightweight CDs or Web site uniform resource locators (URLs).

**CREATIVITY.**   New nonlinear formats and the seamless integration of various media types through multimedia software provide teachers with many ways to be creative in expressing their professional knowledge and skills. This often enables them to highlight their knowledge of how to effectively design instructional materials and blend various sensory stimuli to communicate their ideas and goals. As teachers become more comfortable with multimedia due to the amount of time they spend working with it while creating their digital teaching portfolios, they often discover creative ways to integrate their technical knowledge and skills to develop more creative instruction for their students.

**TECHNOLOGY.**   Digital teaching portfolios are one of the best ways for teachers to communicate their professional use and instructional integration of technology with their teaching. Because of the growing emphasis on technology in classrooms and the increasing number of computers and software in schools, there is a great need for teachers to demonstrate that they can use technology for educational purposes. Digital teaching portfolios make it possible for teachers to provide proof of their technical skills while also displaying their ability to create multimedia presentations, software programs, digital video, and the like.

**SELF-CONFIDENCE.**   The process of creating digital teaching portfolios fosters self-confidence in teachers' own professional abilities. Although traditional teaching portfolios also can help build teachers' self-confidence, preparation of materials in digital format requires them to develop technology knowledge and skills. Learning new techniques, although rewarding on its own, often results in greater self-confidence when teachers recognize their new growth as professionals.

**COMMUNITY.**   Because portfolios in digital format can be easily and inexpensively reproduced and shared on CD or on the World Wide Web, they can be made available locally and globally to viewers around the world and to others in the school community. As a result of this sharing, the creation of digital teaching portfolios can build community among groups that might benefit from such interactions. When sharing portfolios with parents and students, teachers can showcase their professionalism and expertise. When teachers view each other's portfolios, they can build collegiality and gain access to useful ideas and resources. For example, one preservice teacher we worked with included a recycling unit in her digital teaching portfolio and shared it with others online. This preservice teacher learned an important lesson about her own abilities when she received an e-mail from an inservice teacher who had accessed her Web site. This teacher had found her unit and implemented it in her classroom several states away. The preservice teacher's hard work paid off when she learned that students she had never even met had learned a great deal from her innovative work!

## Challenges of Digital Teaching Portfolios

Although there are certainly advantages to digital teaching portfolios, they do present some challenges. In the following sections, we elaborate on some of these challenges.

**KNOWLEDGE AND SKILL REQUIREMENTS.** To create a digital teaching portfolio teachers need advanced knowledge about teaching portfolios in general and digital teaching portfolios in particular, as well as skills in using various hardware and software. Unlike traditional portfolios, the compilation of materials for digital teaching portfolios requires special knowledge about the organization of multimedia materials and graphic design. Inclusion of materials in this type of portfolio requires teachers to convert the format of various artifacts into digital format. To make it even more difficult, different artifacts often require different conversion methods. In cases when teachers do not already possess this knowledge themselves, they require professional support.

**PROFESSIONAL SUPPORT.** Teachers need good teachers if they are going to learn how to create their own digital teaching portfolio. More often than not, school districts lack the professional development personnel required to perform the time-consuming job of aiding teachers with the development of digital portfolios. Even when districts have available staff, the time of these personnel is often spent dealing with issues deemed of "higher priority" by state boards of education and the other bodies that oversee schools. In these situations, schools might use parent or community volunteers as support for teachers, but this approach often can be challenging.

**EXPENSIVE EQUIPMENT.** Even though a teacher might use many different materials to create a traditional teaching portfolio (e.g., paper, binders, felt, ribbons, photographs, index cards, etc.), few of these materials will be as expensive as those required to create a digital teaching portfolio. High-tech equipment comes with an equally high price tag, requires expensive repairs when it breaks down, and becomes obsolete quickly. Even the best equipment breaks, often leaving even the most motivated teacher in a "holding pattern" until it is fixed.

**TIME AND ENERGY.** Digital teaching portfolios require an investment of time and energy before they can become a reality. Teachers must be committed not only to creating a portfolio (which is often a chore in itself), but also to creating one in digital format. Development of a digital teaching portfolio takes even more time than the development of a traditional one—in part because of the learning involved for most teachers and in part because digital portfolios often inspire greater content, creativity, and depth.

**INCREASED VIEWER SKILLS AND EQUIPMENT.**  Using digital teaching portfolios rather than traditional, paper-based ones, also means that the members of the audience will need additional skills and equipment in order to view the portfolio contents. Whereas all principals, employers, teacher educators, and parents can view the contents of a traditional teaching portfolio in a notebook, only those with technical skills and computer equipment can view digital teaching portfolios. Access to digital teaching portfolios can be restricted to parents with education and resources—a situation that can be problematic.

**PRESENTATION THAT DETRACTS FROM CONTENT.**  One additional disadvantage of presenting teaching portfolios in digital format is that the technology can often obstruct the view of teachers' real accomplishments and competence. When too much emphasis is placed on the high-tech "bells and whistles," or when too much information is included, or when insufficient emphasis is placed on the actual content, the artifacts and reflections demonstrating teachers' accomplishments can be overshadowed. Likewise, when teachers have difficulty managing the digital presentation of their work, their expertise and talents can be questioned.

## SUMMARY

Portfolios may be defined as purposeful compilations of and reflections on an individual's work, effort, and progress over time. Portfolios are used in various professions for many reasons and take different forms based on their purpose and audience. Two basic types of portfolios exist: working portfolios and presentation portfolios. Both types have special features and characteristics. A teaching portfolio is a special type of presentation portfolio that functions primarily to demonstrate multiple facets of teaching professionalism.

Digital teaching portfolios are teaching portfolios that integrate technology with the processes of creating a portfolio and the display of the product resulting from this process. Creating a portfolio using digital technologies has a number of advantages. Materials in a digital teaching portfolio can be more accessible than those in traditional portfolios because they can be viewed by multiple users simultaneously, disseminated easily, and reproduced quickly and inexpensively. Digital teaching portfolios can be more portable than more traditional ones if they are stored on a disk or CD. Teachers who use digital tools to create their portfolios often find multimedia environments provide them with a great deal of creative freedom. Also, they frequently say that the process helps them build self-confidence and technical skills. However, creating portfolios in digital format does have some disadvantages. The process requires special knowledge and skill. It also takes time and resources that may not be available to all teachers. In addition, portfolios in digital format can be inaccessible to certain populations who may want to view them if access to necessary hardware and software is not provided.

## CHECK YOUR UNDERSTANDING

1. Describe the different types of portfolios.
2. What factors influence the inclusion of different materials in portfolios?
3. To gain a concrete understanding of what a digital teaching portfolio is and its components, examine the following portfolios online:
   - Russell O. Bean (secondary preservice teacher) at http://www.omnicast.net/users/cckid/about.html
   - Amy Johnson (secondary preservice teacher, UVA) at http://curry.edschool.virginia.edu/curry/class/edlf/589-07/Amy_Johnson
   - Kelly Fischer (elementary preservice teacher) at http://durak.org/kathy/portfolio
   - Carter Shreves (elementary preservice teacher, UVA) at http://curry.edschool.virginia.edu/curry/class/edlf/589-07/Carter_Shreves
   - Kelly Mandia (secondary teacher) at http://www.mandia.com/kelly/portfolio.htm
   - Middle school preservice teacher at http://www2.ncsu.edu/unity/lockers/project/portfolios/presevice1.html
   - National Board Certified Teacher Portfolio Example: Early Adolescence English Language Arts Certification at http://www2.ncsu.edu/unity/lockers/project/portfolios/nbcfile3.html

a. Locate and review additional digital teaching portfolios online by conducting a search using the words "electronic teaching portfolio," "digital teaching portfolio," or "professional portfolio" using any of the following search engines or Web directories:
   - http://www.altavista.com (search engine)
   - http://www.google.com (search engine)
   - http://www.hotbot.com (search engine)
   - http://www.northernlight.com (search engine)
   - http://www.yahoo.com (Web directory)

b. Answer the following questions after reviewing the portfolios:
   - What elements are common among all of the portfolios you have examined?
   - What elements do you think are important to include in your portfolio? Why?
   - Why would you want to create a digital teaching portfolio as opposed to a traditional (print-based) teaching portfolio?
   - What are the advantages and disadvantages of using the World Wide Web to publish a teaching portfolio?

# chapter

## Putting
## Portfolios
## in Perspective

t w o

**B**efore exploring the idea of digital teaching portfolios any further, it is useful to consider two trends influencing the portfolio movement in education. These trends are the increased need for effective measures of educational quality and efforts to enhance teacher professionalism. Considering these trends helps us to understand why digital teaching portfolios are catching on. They make the expenditure of time, effort, and resources required to create one seem practical and wise.

## Standards and the Quest for Educational Quality

What do extensible markup language (XML), gold, the Italian greyhound, and K–12 teachers have in common? All have standards by which they may be measured. Although programming languages, precious metals, canines, and educators are undoubtedly different, all are subject to the scrutiny of different groups—groups of "experts" who proclaim special knowledge about quality and authenticity. So why the need to measure quality and authenticity through standards? Perhaps the movement to develop and use standards is related to the growing number of choices and options in the world today. The more choices we have, the more important it becomes to possess accurate information for making decisions about these choices. In theory, measuring educational quality against standards can provide information that enables people and groups to make good decisions regarding educational choices.

## The Relationship between Choice, Standards, and Quality

The number of options people can choose from when making decisions is growing rapidly in all areas of life. Consider the number of options the average person has when selecting even the most mundane household item—toilet paper! The selection of toilet paper available at the average grocery store is daunting. This product is made by many different companies. It varies in price, thickness, number of sheets, fragrance, texture, and visual pattern. Although this product plays an important part in everyday life, we are fortunate that decisions about toilet paper are not as important and time-consuming as many of the other choices in our lives. Otherwise grocery shopping would take even longer than it already does!

Especially where money is involved, more choice means more difficult and time-consuming decision making. There are more choices in education just as in other areas of life. Those who make decisions about education as individuals or groups have always used information about quality as the basis for decision making. However, concepts of educational quality have changed in the last century due to population growth, economic prosperity, redistribution of wealth, and greater involvement of government in education.

Measuring educational quality with standardized measures is a new phenomenon. Until recently, educational quality was based primarily on reputation. The socioeconomic status of a school's students and alumni, condition of its campus, faculty credentials, religious affiliation, and geographic location all contributed to a school's reputation. By and large, educational quality had more to do with the level of opportunity a student gained through association with a school rather than the extent of knowledge they acquired while attending it.

Changes in the world today have made relying on reputation as a measure of educational quality an impractical method for most decision making. Need and desire for a common measuring stick are behind much of the movement toward standards-based reforms.

Families, communities, businesses, and government groups share the need to determine the quality of educational experiences in different learning environments using a common method of assessment. Parents want to send their children to high-quality schools so they will gain the knowledge and skills that will make them happy and successful adults. Families often choose to live in certain states, cities, and communities based on information gained from measures of educational quality. Communities want to improve poor-quality schools and reward the success of high-quality ones. This helps them to attract residents who will strengthen their community. Businesses want to locate in areas with quality educational offerings. This enables them to attract employees who will contribute to their financial success. Government groups also want to gain information about educational quality. This information can be used to promote equal opportunity for all students.

## Measuring Educational Quality with Standardized Testing

The most common measure of educational quality is student performance on standardized tests that measure student aptitude, knowledge, and skills. The result of student performance on these tests is then compared at state and national levels through a process called standardization. The publication of *A Nation at Risk* (National Commission on Excellence in Education, NCEE 1983) marked the beginning of the movement to measure quality using tests with standardized scores—or standardized tests. The report advocated higher standards for all, suggesting that standardized tests should be given to students at regular levels throughout their schooling (NCEE, 1983). Almost twenty years later, media sources ranging from local headlines to national reports use standardized tests to gauge educational quality.

Parents commonly make use of standardized test results to determine which school districts are the most desirable places to live and work. Local school boards use such information to gauge the quality of educational offerings in their districts. At the state and national levels, standardized test scores influence decisions regarding funding and governance. This information also is used to compare the quality of educational offerings across school districts, to discern the influence of funding and demographics on student success, and to determine the worthiness of various government-funded programs.

Despite the widespread use of this information as a measure of educational quality, it is problematic for at least two major reasons. First, it presumes that students' aptitude, knowledge, and skills can be accurately measured by their performance on standardized tests. Second, it assumes that educational quality can be gauged by this limited indicator when educational quality is a composite of many different factors.

Reliance on such information, as faulty as it may be, occurs for several reasons. One reason is that information about student performance on norm-referenced, standardized tests is available on a wide scale. The universal availability of such information makes educational comparisons across states and school districts possible even though considerable variation exists among them. The easy administration of such tests, their utility in organizing curriculum offerings, and their relatively low cost make them popular assessment tools. Another reason that this information is used as a measure of educational quality is because it is quantitative. Because student performance on standardized tests can be expressed easily using numbers and analyzed using statistical tests, it has the advantage of communicating information about exceptionally large student populations. Quantitative expressions such as mean, median, mode, and standard deviation can be communicated economically without requiring the incredible volume of information necessary to explain qualitative information. A final reason this information is used so commonly as a measure of educational quality is because such information has become popularly accepted. Parents, politicians, and the media have learned what these standardized measures mean and have come to accept them as a valid and reliable indicator of educational quality. Whether it makes sense or not, standardized testing information has been used for so long that most decision-makers feel comfortable describing educational quality this way.

Until recently, the ideas, tools, and leaders needed to develop, implement, analyze, and communicate more accurate measures of educational quality were not available. But, advances in human thinking and technology suggest that eventually it may be possible to better gauge educational quality through an examination of multiple indicators, such as teacher quality, curriculum offerings, community involvement, and various factors relating to student performance. The authentic assessment movement is led by individuals who strive toward this goal by advocating more accurate measures of educational quality through student and teacher performance. Portfolios play an important role in this movement.

## The Push for Authentic Assessment

The goal of authentic assessment is to measure individual performance or achievement in situations or tasks that most closely match the challenges and standards of real life. The idea behind this practice is that the best indicator of students' and educators' level of achievement is performance on the tasks for which educational or professional experiences are supposed to prepare them. When portfolios are used as the basis for assessment, progress on real-world tasks (e.g., writing, solving problems, developing projects) can enable the tracking of growth over time and help individuals learn to assess their own progress against standards of quality. More and more educators are using portfolios as an alternative form of student assessment because multiple-choice tests, which despite their ease in creation, administration, and grading, are inadequate measures of what students know and can do. More and more school districts are using portfolios to assess teacher achievement because measures of student performance are not enough.

If accurate evaluation is the strength of authentic assessment, consistent evaluation is its greatest weakness. Applying a standard rubric to the evaluation of authentic performance requires a unified vision of what student or teacher performance means in fifty states and countless school districts. For the moment, such a rubric eludes even the best and brightest leaders in the field.

## Enhancing Teacher Professionalism

Measuring the quality of teaching, as in evaluating the quality of any other artistic endeavor such as painting, sculpture, and dance, is a difficult business. Three national professional associations representing the "three-legged stool of teacher quality" (National Commission on Teaching and America's Future 1996, p. 29), the National Board for Professional Teaching Standards (NBPTS), the Interstate New Teacher Assessment and Support Consortium (INTASC), and the National Council for the Accreditation of Teacher Education (NCATE), have come to agreement on what constitutes high levels of teacher performance. A fourth professional organization, the International Society for Technology in Education (ISTE), also has developed standards for teachers. The development of nationally recognized standards and their application in the use of portfolios provides new ways to measure quality of education and teaching. It also has enhanced understanding of teacher professionalism.

## Professional Standards

In this section, we present a brief description of the various professional organizations that have developed professional standards and provide a short summary of each set of standards. Although constituent groups of the different organizations and reasons for the development of standards vary, their aims overlap considerably. Later we explain how and why these standards could serve as the framework for the creation of a digital teaching portfolio.

NBPTS (http://www.nbpts.org), an association composed primarily of classroom teachers, administrators, and other education professionals, is the most notable organizatin to develop a set of standards expressing what accomplished teachers should know and be able to do. The standards address five core propositions for how accomplished teachers demonstrate their level of knowledge, skills, abilities, and commitment. These propositions suggest (NBPTS, 2001):

1. Teachers are committed to students and their learning.
2. Teachers know the subjects they teach and how to teach those subjects to students.
3. Teachers are responsible for managing and monitoring student learning.
4. Teachers think systematically about their practice and learn from experience.
5. Teachers are members of learning communities.

INTASC (http://www.ccsso.org/intascst.html) is a program of the Council of Chief State School Officers. Members of the consortium consist of representatives from the teaching profession, as well as personnel from seventeen state education agencies. This group developed performance-based standards representing a common core of teaching knowledge and skills that all beginning teachers, regardless of their area of specialty, should be able to demonstrate. These standards were designed to be compatible with those developed by the NBPTS but target beginning teachers. The INTASC principles build upon NBPTS's core propositions; they are (Darling-Hammond, 1992):

1. The teacher understands the central concepts, tools of inquiry, and structures of the discipline(s) he or she teaches and can create learning experiences that make these aspects of subject matter meaningful for students.

2. The teacher understands how children learn and develop and can provide learning opportunities that support their intellectual, social, and personal development.

3. The teacher understands how students differ in their approaches to learning and creates instructional opportunities that are adapted to diverse learners.

4. The teacher understands and uses a variety of instructional strategies to encourage students' development of critical thinking, problem solving, and performance skills.

5. The teacher uses an understanding of individual and group motivation and behavior to create a learning environment that encourages positive social interaction, active engagement in learning, and self-motivation.

6. The teacher uses knowledge of effective verbal, nonverbal, and media communication techniques to foster active inquiry, collaboration, and supportive interaction in the classroom.

7. The teacher plans instruction based upon knowledge of subject matter, students, the community, and curriculum goals.

8. The teacher understands and uses formal and informal assessment strategies to evaluate and ensure the continuous intellectual, social, and physical development of the learner.

9. The teacher is a reflective practitioner who continually evaluates the effects of his/her choices and actions on others (students, parents, and other professionals in the learning community) and who actively seeks out opportunities to grow professionally.

10. The teacher fosters relationships with school colleagues, parents, and agencies in the larger community to support students' learning and well-being.

NCATE (http://www.ncate.org) is made up of a coalition of thirty-three specialty professional associations of teachers, teacher educators, content specialists, and local and state policy makers committed to improving the quality of teacher preparation in the United States. NCATE's main purpose as an independent agency is to improve the quality of professional preparation by providing professional accreditation to schools, colleges, and departments of education (referred to in the standards as units). This organization developed standards to serve as the basis of a voluntary, peer-reviewed process. NCATE's (2001a) accreditation standards are:

1. **Candidate knowledge, skills, and dispositions.** Candidates preparing to work in schools as teachers or other professional school personnel know and demonstrate the content, pedagogical, and professional knowledge, skills, and dispositions necessary to help all students learn. Assessments indicate that candidates meet professional, state, and institutional standards.

2. **Assessment system and unit evaluation.** The unit has an assessment system that collects and analyzes data on applicant qualifications, candidate and graduate performance, and unit operations to evaluate and improve the unit and its programs.

3. **Field experiences and clinical practice.** The unit and its school partners design, implement, and evaluate field experiences and clinical practice so that teacher candidates and other school personnel develop and demonstrate the knowledge, skills, and dispositions necessary to help all students learn.

4. **Diversity.** The unit designs, implements, and evaluates curriculum and experiences for candidates to acquire and apply the knowledge, skills, and dispositions necessary to help all students learn. These experiences include working with diverse higher education and school faculty, diverse candidates, and diverse students in P–12 schools.

5. **Faculty qualifications, performance, and development.** Faculty are qualified and model best professional practices in scholarship, service, and teaching, including the assessment of their own effectiveness as related to candidate performance. They also collaborate with colleagues in the disciplines and schools. The unit systematically evaluates faculty performance and facilitates professional development.

6. **Unit governance and resources.** The unit has the leadership, authority, budget, personnel, facilities, and resources, including information technology resources, for the preparation of candidates to meet professional, state, and institutional standards.

NCATE measures the knowledge and skills teaching candidates exhibit during and after program completion, with standards developed for seventeen specfic professional areas. Constituent organizations, representing different professional areas develop program standards communicating what candidates should know and be able to do as a result of participation in courses and other experiences units provide. A listing of NCAT$E constituent organizations and links to the various standards are provided at http://www.ncate.org/ncate/conslist.htm

ISTE (http://www.iste.org), a group made up of educators, teacher educators, and other technology users, issued a set of national educational technology standards for all teachers in July 2000. Although the focus of these standards is on preservice teachers, the standards also provide guidelines for inservice teachers currently in the classroom. ISTE's (2000c) standards have twenty-three indicators organized around the following six categories:

1. Technology Operations and Concepts
2. Planning and Designing Learning Environments and Experiences
3. Teaching, Learning, and Curriculum
4. Assessment and Evaluation
5. Productivity and Professional Practice
6. Social, Ethical, Legal, and Human Issues

## Professional Standards and Digital Teaching Portfolios

It is important to note that all of the aforementioned standards and the professional groups who created them are supportive of portfolios. Each group recognizes the role teaching portfolios can play in demonstrating the attainment of standards and enhancing professionalism. Both traditional and digital portfolios are recognized as being useful for this purpose.

The NBPTS has been instrumental in promoting the use of teaching portfolios as a tool for measuring teacher quality and enhancing teachers' level of professionalism. This group requires teachers seeking national certification to submit portfolios to assessors for examination. NBPTS requires that an applicant's portfolio demonstrate evidence of teacher competence in a variety of formats, including a lesson captured on videotape. At present, they do not require that an entire portfolio be presented in digital format.

ISTE includes the creation of digital teaching portfolios in its standards explicitly. In Professional Preparation Performance Profile Standard 15, it suggests that all preservice teachers should, "develop a portfolio of technology-based products from coursework, including the related assessment tools" (ISTE 2000a). Creation of a digital portfolio is expected as a demonstration of competence in two of six standards categories: Assessment and Evaluation (IV) and Productivity and Professional Practice (V).

NCATE's accreditation system has progressed to a performance-based system of accreditation—a natural fit for the use of portfolios. As such, it supports students' creation of portfolios and their use as evaluative tools. In the past, NCATE has used a variety of measures to determine the degree to which teacher preparation programs demonstrate the attainment of accreditation standards. However, in the newest set of guidelines, performance-based evaluation is more important than ever before (NCATE 2001a). For institutions to earn accreditation, they "must demonstrate that candidates know their subject and how to teach it effectively so that students learn" (NCATE 2001b). This change in the new guidelines has motivated teacher preparation institutions that desire NCATE accreditation to begin incorporating students' creation of digital teaching portfolios for the purpose of showcasing teachers' professional knowledge and skills.

## Creating Standards-Based Teaching Portfolios

Even if teachers and the organizations associated with them (e.g., schools of education, school districts, individual schools) are not motivated by the official rewards that recognition from groups such as NBPTS, INTASC, NCATE, and ISTE offer they may still choose to design a digital teaching portfolio responsive to standards due to other rewards it can bring. Those who strive to create portfolios based on these standards may benefit in other ways. First, they will likely improve their teaching practice by taking the time to reflect on their accomplishments in various professional domains. Second, regardless of which standards they utilize, they will create a collection of work that is based on teaching accomplishments that are nationally recognized. This means that the portfolio will have national credibility regardless of the geographic location where a portfolio is displayed. Other benefits resulting from digital teaching portfolios in general (as opposed to those created in response to professional standards) are communicated in Chapter 3.

## Implications of Standards-Based Teaching Portfolios for Measuring Educational Quality

The standards created by professional groups and their use in the formation and evaluation of digital teaching portfolios are important to our discussion of educational quality for several reasons. First, the development of standards that are accepted nationally suggests that it may eventually be possible to arrive at a nationally accepted method for generating information about teacher quality. This information will be useful in helping families and government officials make better decisions about educational quality. Second, the efforts put forth by these organizations and the resulting standards suggest that it is indeed possible for groups of people concerned with education to come together, create, and define common expectations for what constitutes high-quality performance. Third, it indicates the development of authentic assessments for measuring quality is possible. If nationally recognized standards for high-quality teacher performance can be developed and authentic methods of evaluating them implemented, then perhaps it may be possible to develop the same for students so that better information about educational quality can be obtained for decision making.

## SUMMARY

In this chapter, we considered some of the reasons that portfolios for teachers and students are becoming used more widely across the United States. We explored the relationship between choice, educational quality, standards, and assessment. As the number of educational options has expanded, so has the need for more dependable and reliable measures of educational quality. Information about academic quality is needed and desired by families, communities, businesses, and the government for many different reasons. The practice of measuring educational quality by comparing student performance on standardized tests was described as a common practice with many limitations. Although the method allows comparison of student performance that is accepted by many, possibly on a large scale, and across many states, such a measure is limited in its ability to measure educational quality. Such measures fail to estimate teacher quality—a key component of educational quality. And they provide only one measure of student learning. Alternative assessment, often called authentic assessment because it gauges individual accomplishment on tasks more closely tied to performance-based measures in the real world, was suggested as a better measure of educational quality. Proponents of authentic assessment advocate the use of portfolios with students and teachers because they have the ability to demonstrate performance on many meaningful tasks. However, a method for the valid, reliable, and generalizable measurement of educational quality through the evaluation of portfolios has not been developed yet. Various professional organizations advocate the use of portfolios to enhance the professionalism of teachers. These groups include INTASC, NBPTS, ISTE, and NCATE. All of these groups recommend the use of portfolios to demonstrate attainment of professional standards. ISTE includes the creation of a digital portfolio in its list of standards that demonstrate competence.

## CHECK YOUR UNDERSTANDING

1. What is the most common information used to measure educational quality? What are the problems with using this information?
2. What is authentic assessment?
3. How might standards improve teacher performance?
4. What professional organizations have standards for teachers that might be used for developing portfolios?

# The Benefits of Digital Teaching Portfolios for Preservice and Inservice Teachers

## three

We could not write a book about digital teaching portfolios if we did not believe there were many benefits that result from creating them. In Chapters 3 and 4 we discuss the positive things that can happen when different individuals and groups invest time and energy in creating digital teaching portfolios. Teachers at every career stage, whether preservice or inservice, can benefit directly through portfolio creation. In addition, the parents and students with whom teachers work benefit indirectly from their portfolios.

## Professional Benefits for Teachers

It is ironic that teachers, who focus so much time and energy on their students' growth and development, have little time and energy to focus on their own. During the 1994–1995 school year, teachers spent an average of forty-two hours on professional development—a relatively small number of hours considering the number of hours the average teacher spends on the job (1,440; 8 hours per day, 180 each year) (Alexander, Heaviside, and Farris, 1998).

Both the process involved in creating a digital teaching portfolio and the product that results from it have value for teachers. Teachers who create portfolios often have increased self-esteem, energy levels, and enthusiasm. The portfolio process also can lead to improved working conditions if learning is centered on the classroom environment. Portfolios that teachers create also are valuable when used to communicate teacher competence and professionalism to a school community. Here we describe just a few personal and professional gains derived from digital teaching portfolios and the portfolio creation process. The remainder of this text often adopts the use of the terms *digital portfolio* or *portfolio* to indicate teaching portfolios created in digital format.

## Creation of Digital Teaching Portfolios Makes Teachers Learners

In our opinion, the most compelling reason for involving teachers in creating digital teaching portfolios is overlooked in the literature on this form of professional development. Surprisingly, few portfolio advocates recognize that something wonderful occurs when teachers are involved in the learning processes required to create digital teaching portfolios—teachers get the chance to become learners. During the portfolio creation process, teachers learn about themselves, their profession, and new technologies. Most important, they experience again what it feels like to be a learner. They are reintroduced to the dilemmas and delights of the learning process. What better experience could there be to increase teachers' empathy with their students!

Teachers, like most adults, rarely have the opportunity to put themselves in environments where they are totally immersed as learners—exposed to completely new vocabulary, concepts, and conventions. It is hard to find environments where adults' prior knowledge is useless. We have observed that plunging teachers into a learning environment can provide them with important new insights and old understandings long forgotten, resulting in better teachers.

One early childhood educator we worked with learned a simple programming language called hypertext mark-up language (HTML) in the process of creating her digital teaching portfolio. In a journal reflection, she commented on how this experience was like learning to read. In this quote she indicates that the process gave her a better understanding of what it is like to be a learner and a new understanding of the stages involved in literacy.

> Learning HTML is very similar to learning to read in that HTML is a language all of its own. When people learn how to use HTML, they become immersed in a language of symbols and protocols that can be very complicated and confusing—just like when a child is learning to read. The child may have had some exposure to certain symbols representing particular letters, but they need to learn about how all these symbols need to be assem-

bled in order to form words. If they don't arrange the letters in a particular order, the meaning is changed completely or doesn't make any sense at all. Just like when a person is learning how to write HTML. In the same way, a child can change the meaning of a word by omitting or adding a letter, those learning html can make their message completely inaccessible by misplacing a letter or symbol.

A child can learn to read by repeated exposure to words and their meaning with the aid of a teacher, parent, or another literate helper. An adult or older child can learn HTML by taking classes, reading manuals, and through trial and error. Once they understand how to diagnose their own difficulties, they are "literate" in the HTML world and no longer need an official teacher. Once children learn how to read they will understand that certain orders of letters indicate specific meaning. They will be able to continuously read words that they know and also be able to string together new words by combining the words that they know.

As evidenced by this reflection, it is reasonable to think that total immersion in the learning process can be a good thing for teachers and their students.

Any mention of teachers becoming learners must be tempered with a cautionary message. Learners, especially adult learners, have special needs; are vulnerable; and require appropriate human, instructional, and technical support. One student explained the experience of learning to create a portfolio this way,

> My experience was like running a marathon. Along the way, there were various problems I encountered. At one point, I did not think I had the capacity to be running the race. At another, I fell down and damaged my pride. If I hadn't found the support I needed with my instructor cheering me on and handing me a cold glass of water, I would have dropped out of the running altogether.

## Digital Teaching Portfolios Provide Opportunities to Learn About Technology

The creation of digital teaching portfolios can act as a catalyst for teacher development in the area of technology. During the portfolio production process, teachers have legitimate reasons to use technology equipment in meaningful ways. They have motivation to experiment with different types of hardware (computers, digital cameras, scanners, video cameras) and software (image creation and manipulation software, Web editing software) and develop new knowledge and skills. By creating digital teaching portfolios, teachers put their knowledge and learning to the test by combining technology skills with their professional knowledge to create a tangible product. In addition, the creation of a digital teaching portfolio can address several of the critical domains (ISTE 2000b) in which teachers must be fluent, according to national professional associations.

## Digital Teaching Portfolios Improve Teachers' Impact on Students

Although the notion that a student's use of technology improves their learning is long on anecdotal evidence and short on hard data, we believe a teacher's experience with technology, such as what they gain in the digital portfolio process, can improve student learning in several ways. First, teachers who create their own digital teaching portfolios become aware of the potential that technology has for enabling the creative process. Gaining an opportunity to demonstrate their own knowledge with a variety of media, they understand the value of representing learning and growth in the well-rounded ways that digital media enables. Teachers who see how their own skills and knowledge can be demonstrated in various mediums are more likely to provide their students this opportunity. Second, teachers who have created their own portfolios might provide their students the chance to create digital learning portfolios or simply to look for multiple indicators of learning. Third, the technical skills that teachers develop by creating a digital teaching portfolio can be put to use to improve teaching and learning. Teachers who use multimedia to create instructional materials can help students by presenting information in more efficient, effective, and engaging ways.

## Digital Teaching Portfolios Are Effective Tools for Demonstrating Teacher Competence

Portfolios are a powerful way for teachers to demonstrate their professional competence to others. Whether the "others" include prospective employers, school parents, or state certification officers, the artifacts included in a teacher's portfolio can speak volumes about her proficiency in areas such as curriculum planning, instruction, home–school communication, and professional knowledge. After all, what better way to "show your stuff" than to actually show your stuff!

Many states now require teachers to submit portfolios for initial and advanced certification. Methods for assessing portfolios are being developed that promise to provide those interested in measuring teacher quality an alternative, and perhaps superior, way than that demonstrated by student performance on standardized tests. In a time when credibility of and respect for educators is diminishing, the promotion of information about teacher quality is of great importance. Teachers' professional competence and expertise need to be displayed for all to see. Digital teaching portfolios can be shared with the community, parents, and colleagues online in relatively convenient and inexpensive ways.

## Digital Teaching Portfolios Help Teachers Get Jobs

The trend of dragging weighty binders and notebooks along to job interviews has been building since the late 1980s. However, in these days of personal digital assistants and laptop computers, heavy, oversized reference items no longer guarantee the "edge" they did in the past. Merely having a portfolio is no longer good enough. Despite the "teacher shortage" and proliferation of teaching positions in some regions of the United States, when teachers compete for prized jobs, every advantage counts. Today's employers are looking for technologically savvy teachers. Even when teachers create the most simple of digital portfolios, the fact that their credentials appear in multimedia format communicate their willingness to innovate, their interest in developing new skills, and their effort to appear professional. For teachers who are highly skilled and technologically sophisticated, digital teaching portfolios offer the only way for them to showcase the instructional materials they have created with technology. After all, you cannot demonstrate multimedia expertise with a pencil and paper!

## Digital Teaching Portfolios Are More Portable

Digital teaching portfolios are more practical and convenient than traditional portfolios for several reasons. First, they are lightweight and easy to carry. Teachers who are interviewing can postpone toting their large oversized tote bags until after they get a teaching job! Second, digital teaching portfolios preserve precious, often irreplaceable, primary-source materials. Let's face it. If students' lunch money is not secure in schools, neither is a teacher's portfolio. In the past, when a job candidate wanted to provide a school administrator time to review their credentials, the candidate left the only original copy at the school for a while because there was no alternative. This is no longer the case. Using digital technology to create a teaching portfolio makes it possible to scan and make copies of artifacts. This makes the artifacts safer and more accessible. Portfolios in digital format can be burned on CD-ROM and reproduced inexpensively or presented on the Web, both methods allow the port-folio to be disseminated widely.

There is still a place for portfolios produced in traditional formats. We suggest that this place is in teachers' classrooms where students and visiting parents can review their teachers' accomplishments in hard-copy form. In classrooms where students are encouraged to create portfolios, a teacher's portfolio carries more than a message about the teacher's competence. The mere presence of a teacher's portfolio acts as an endorsement for students' participation in this vital learning experience. After teachers are finished making digital copies of the hard evidence in their portfolios, the original work should take a place of honor.

## Digital Teaching Portfolios Are a Tool for Charting Future Professional Growth

Digital teaching portfolios may act as springboards for future professional development. Digital portfolios are biographical in that they provide a snapshot of a teacher's competence over a certain period of time. By creating and examining a portfolio, teachers can reflect upon past and present accomplishments as well as what they still wish to accomplish in the future. Along these lines, teachers allow educators to reexamine their beliefs and philosophies over time, allowing them to see how they have grown professionally and philosophically. Teachers also can create a digital teaching portfolio that includes a plan for professional development. As time progresses, teachers can refer to the portfolio to see if they have stayed on course with this plan. Finally, by examining portfolios, both teachers and other personnel (such as the principal) can help determine teachers' needs for professional growth and how to achieve it. For example, a teacher might have a great deal of supporting data for several standards, but not much for one of them. The standard that has not been adequately addressed in the portfolio may be an area in which the teacher might want to invest some time.

# Personal Benefits for Teachers

Separating the personal and professional dimensions of teaching can be quite difficult. In fact, many good teachers make no division between these dimensions. Perhaps this is one reason that being a good teacher is so exhausting! Yet, when discussing the benefits of digital teaching portfolios, we feel it worth mentioning that there are benefits that influence a person's well being and happiness separate from their role as a teacher.

## Digital Teaching Portfolios Promote a Sense of Accomplishment and Satisfaction

Many teachers experience a great deal of satisfaction with their work (they must, otherwise, why would they work so hard for so little pay?). Creating a portfolio results in a tangible product that can boost teacher satisfaction. The following vignette from one of our classes describes a class session in which a student shares her portfolio-in-progress, demonstrating her confidence and satisfaction in her abilities to use technology.

> It's 1:02 PM. All of the students have arrived on time except for Mark who is in New Jersey on a job interview. As Patricia sits down, she tells Karen that she needs to show her the latest changes to her Web-based portfolio. Karen chuckles, and tells one of the instructors, "Patricia is always showing everyone her Web page. She shows it to our sorority sisters, to her boyfriend, even my parents who came to visit last weekend." Patricia taps Karen on the shoulder in a chiding way, and beams, "I just get so excited with what I've put together."
>
> Patricia accesses her digital portfolio on the computer and shows Karen how she has restructured her Web page to have frames. "That way, my site is much more organized. All you have to do is click on the left and you get whatever you clicked on the right," says Patricia. "Wow, how did you do that?" asks Karen. At the same time, Paul, Ann, and Cassidy move toward Patricia's seat to look over her shoulder. Larry and Sharon remain at their

seats since they are trying to figure out why one of Larry's graphics is not showing up. Melissa, one of the instructors of the class, then asks Patricia if she would share her portfolio with the class and how she organized it.

Patricia gets up and moves to the presentation computer to share the recent changes in her portfolio. She explains that she decided to use frames with her portfolio because it allows her to better organize all of the information she wants to put up. For instance, she wants to include an introduction, her educational philosophy, her resume, her educational background, and a section on curriculum and instruction, as well as future goals and educational history. Using frames allows her to organize it so that her page is easy to navigate.

When Patricia finishes sharing her portfolio, one student asks, "How hard was it to do that?" Patricia answered, "It wasn't easy, but it wasn't really hard either. Look, if I can do this, I know you can! At the beginning of the semester I never would have dreamed that I could even create a Web page, and look at all I have done—all that all of us have done! We can create Web pages, upload and download them, convert graphics, scan pictures, all kinds of stuff that most of us couldn't do before this class. So, what I'm saying is that it isn't easy, but I know you can do it."

## Digital Teaching Portfolios Are Evidence of Personal Growth

Some parents make a habit of recording their children's heights periodically on a doorframe or wall in their homes. Those who do are aware of the proud feelings their children experience when looking over the successive marks recording their physical growth. Portfolios, for many teachers, become equally effective ways to measure personal growth. From what we can tell, teachers who use this method of recording their growth experience tremendous satisfaction when they behold their finished portfolios. Teaching portfolios created in digital format have the advantage of recording even more benchmarks for teachers because the amount of storage space is almost infinite. Because they demonstrate growth data over a long period of time, digital portfolios can be an even greater source of satisfaction.

## Skills Learned in Creating Digital Teaching Portfolios Have Personal Applications

Many teachers we know have put the skills they developed when creating digital teaching portfolios to work for themselves outside of school for personal reasons. What better proof that the technical skills many teachers pick up during the portfolio creation process are enjoyable and fun! One fourth-grade teacher who learned how to put her portfolio onto the Internet used her skills to create a Web site for a friend's wedding. Not only did she save money on a wedding gift, she made it possible for the bride and her family to share important travel information with their guests. Another teacher used her skills to create a multimedia CD containing her family history that included family photos, videos, and sound files. Her family was delighted when she distributed her creation as a holiday present to her large family.

In many cases, teachers devote more time applying the skills they learn to personal rather than professional use. Maybe this is because people are often more invested in personal projects than professional ones. Or perhaps it is due to the fact that personal projects rarely have stringent deadlines and other time constraints. Regardless, the skills acquired during personal experimentation can be applied for both personal and professional dimensions.

Teachers with whom we have worked have proven that their skills are also financially valuable. Some teachers have secured summer and part-time work doing multimedia development and Web design for small businesses such as real estate offices and travel agencies. Others have found the digital teaching portfolio process to be life-altering. They discovered new talents and interests when developing their digital portfolios and ended up pursuing advanced degrees in instructional design and technology-related fields.

## SUMMARY

In this chapter, we discussed some of the benefits that can result from creating a digital teaching portfolio. Teachers benefit both professionally and personally from the portfolio creation process. Engaging in the process of creating a portfolio means teachers must learn about themselves and their work. This makes teachers learners again, which makes them more empathetic, better teachers. Creation of a portfolio using digital tools also enables teachers to develop technical skills and knowledge. Teachers who learn to create their own digital portfolio can do the same with their students, who will undoubtedly benefit from the process. In addition, the portfolio creation process can help teachers market their own competence and chart their professional growth. Personally, teachers can gain a great sense of satisfaction from collecting and displaying their hard work, knowledge, and growth. They can use their newfound skills to create exciting products for personal use, get extra work, or grow in new directions.

## CHECK YOUR UNDERSTANDING

1. In what ways can teachers benefit professionally from creating digital teaching portfolios?

2. In what ways can teachers benefit personally from creating digital teaching portfolios?

# The Benefits

four

4

# of Digital Teaching Portfolios for Principals, School Districts, and Teacher Education Programs

The first time we taught a class on digital teaching portfolios, we wanted the world to experience our students' final portfolio presentations. In the end, we had to settle for anybody we could coax to show up for brownies, lemon bars, cookies, soda, and the promise of an interesting, innovative session. Fortunately, the teacher education faculty we invited as well as the principals and teachers from nearby school districts were successfully lured by these sweets and attended the student presentations. We were not surprised to discover during the discussions that ensued during the consumption of goodies that everyone was very impressed with both the lemon bars and the digital teaching portfolios students had created. However, we were surprised by some of the intriguing perspectives on the value of portfolios offered by our guests that we had never considered. Although our belief that digital teaching portfolios were beneficial to teachers had inspired the class, what we learned about how digital teaching portfolios might benefit school administrators and the organizations with which preservice and inservice teachers are associated inspired this chapter.

Here we present the benefits of digital teaching portfolios for principals and organizations that prepare, certify, and employ teachers. First, we describe some of the ways that digital teaching portfolios created by teachers can benefit principals, schools, and school districts, suggesting a strategy of portfolio-centered professional development that addresses many of the problems associated with professional development. We also describe some of the ways organizations responsible for teacher preparation and certification can gain from implementing digital teaching portfolios and suggest some concrete plans for how this might be done.

# Benefits of Digital Teaching Portfolios for Principals

If a picture speaks a thousand words, how many words are spoken of teachers' credentials if they are communicated digitally in pictures, videos, and other artifacts? We think enough words to indicate whether a principal should employ the teacher or not! Portfolios have long been a favorite professional tool for principals interviewing candidates for teaching positions. Some principals enjoy them so much that they require them of the teachers who work for them and even create their own digital principal portfolios (see Appendix A for information on digital principal portfolios).

## Digital Teaching Portfolios Provide Well-Rounded Proof of Teacher Competence

Digital teaching portfolios provide principals with concrete proof of a candidate's qualifications. In the past, principals made hiring decisions that influenced the lives of many students and their families for the 180-day school year based on several limited documents, such as transcripts, teaching certifications, letters of recommendation, and teaching evaluations. Today, digital teaching portfolios provide a well-rounded set of authentic indicators by which to determine a candidate's competence in addition to the traditional measures typically used.

More telling than scores on the Praxis test or grades in professional coursework are the collection of teaching evaluations, parent letters, lesson plans, and student work presented in digital teaching portfolios. Digital teaching portfolios make it possible to communicate professional competency in more breadth and depth than even traditional portfolios can. Should there be any question about the authenticity of a candidate's credentials, the many materials included in a portfolio enable triangulation and cross-referencing.

### Digital Teaching Portfolios Demonstrate Teachers' Technical Knowledge and Skill

Digital teaching portfolios also are illustrative of a teacher's technical competence. They demonstrate in detail the range of a teacher's knowledge about and skill with technological tools. When a principal reviews a portfolio created in digital format, the principal can determine how well a teacher can use multimedia as a teaching tool. After all, a portfolio is really a lesson about a teacher's professional credentials. How well a teacher can organize information, integrate multimedia, and effectively communicate his or her ideas becomes remarkably clear as a principal clicks through digital materials. Because the ability to use available tools for instructional purposes is highly valued in contemporary classrooms, this information is of great importance to principals. If teachers wish to showcase software or other high-tech instructional materials they have developed for educational purposes, there is no better way to do this than to put it in digital format.

# Benefits of Digital Teaching Portfolios for School Districts

Support from school districts greatly increases the likelihood that teachers will have rewarding experiences while developing their digital teaching portfolios. School districts can foster the development of portfolios if they can provide proper equipment, technical support, and incentives that teachers rely on to maximize their investment of time and energy. Here we present several reasons why school districts will want to consider initiating portfolio development processes for the faculty members they employ. The teachers reading this book should feel free to use these reasons when rallying district support for their efforts!

It also must be noted that centering professional development on the development of digital teaching portfolios might help school districts deal with the major professional development problems of time, travel, and transfer. See Appendix B for more on this topic.

### School Districts Benefit when Teachers Experience the Power of Digital Teaching Portfolio Development

Teachers who create their own digital teaching portfolios experience first-hand the benefits their students might experience if they do the same. Teachers who have created a digital teaching portfolio recognize the ways that student self-esteem can be positively influenced by collecting, selecting, and reflecting on artifacts that display personal growth and development. They also understand how important it is for students to share the fruit of their labors with others in this way.

## School Districts Benefit when Teachers Understand the Role of Digital Teaching Portfolios in Authentic Assessment

In school districts where student portfolios are used as a means of authentic assessment, teacher involvement in the development of digital teaching portfolios is critical. The creation of student portfolios can be time and labor intensive. As such, it requires 100 percent teacher participation, and teachers must often be willing to develop new skills and competencies to support student initiatives. Once teachers have created their own digital teaching portfolios, they are much more likely to "buy in" to district efforts targeting students. In addition, they will understand first-hand the strengths and weaknesses of digital teaching portfolios as an assessment tool. Teachers who have created digital teaching portfolios for their own evaluation can understand how rubrics might be developed to illustrate learning as it is related to real-world tasks and outcomes. Teachers whose performance is evaluated through digital teaching portfolios are more likely to understand and support nontraditional measures of educational quality and student learning district-wide. They are generally more educated and enthusiastic of school efforts.

## School Districts Benefit when Teachers Develop Technical Skills from Creating Digital Teaching Portfolios

School districts in which teachers create portfolios in digital format have teachers who possess technical skills that can be used to enhance instruction. Of course, the fact that teachers have technology skills does not guarantee that they will know how to integrate these skills with instruction. The proper support from professional development staff can enable teachers who have created digital teaching portfolios to improve teaching and learning through the integration of technology. For example, teachers who have learned HTML to create a portfolio to share on the Web can then use this skill to create all kinds of creative, educational materials for their students. Whether WebQuests, classroom newspapers, or homework Web pages, teachers who invest the time in developing competencies with software will find many of ways to use their new skills for their students' benefit.

## School Districts Benefit when Teachers Learn to Chart Their Own Professional Growth with Digital Teaching Portfolios

One last benefit experienced by school districts in which teachers create digital teaching portfolios is that their teachers are likely to develop the ability to reflect on and direct their own professional growth. Because the portfolio process involves many activities that allow teachers to collect, select, and reflect on their professional competencies as they relate to local, state, and national standards, teachers with portfolios have a greater awareness of their strengths and weaknesses. This knowledge makes teachers better able to take advantage of professional development opportunities offered by school districts. It makes them happier, more vital teachers and improves the educational environments of students in the districts in which they work.

# Benefits of Digital Teaching Portfolios for Teacher Education Programs

Across the United States, some 1,300 programs prepare teachers for work in K–12 schools. In these programs, certification candidates are provided with experiences that enable them to develop knowledge and build skills to use in the classroom. Implementing initiatives that enable candidates to create digital teaching portfolios as a part of their professional preparation can result in various positive outcomes for both certification candidates and teacher education programs.

## Digital Teaching Portfolios Help Schools of Education Deal with Issues of Accountability

Reflecting the national preoccupation with educational accountability, new guidelines developed by the NCATE and many state departments of education challenge teacher preparation programs in institutions of higher education to become more accountable for the performance of candidates seeking professional certification for a longer period ot time. Although professional testing through exams taken during participation in teacher education programs such as the National Teacher Examination and Praxis has long been the norm, a new wave of reform is advocating more authentic and continuous assessment of candidates' development throughout the duration of professional education programs and beyond. If trends continue in the current direction, that prepare teachers will be expected to track and be accountable for their candidate's performance as teachers many years after program completion. In response to mandates for continuing assessment, many teacher education programs have implemented portfolio requirements.

Although implementation of portfolio assessment varies, programs generally require preservice teacher candidates to select representative samples of their work during each year of their professional preparation and compile these in portfolios. Each year, program personnel review candidates' portfolios. These reviews are used to determine whether candidates may continue in the program or not. Their portfolios contain indicators of performance on traditional measures of achievement such as position papers and course grades, as well as more authentic items demonstrating knowledge and skills necessary for teaching such as PowerPoint presentations and lesson plans. Oftentimes work is collected in hard-copy format each year and then digitized and organized during a capstone class offered during candidates' last semester. The final digital portfolio often is used in the job placement process.

Because digital teaching portfolios present a wide array of materials, more information is available to faculty members about teacher candidates' performance. This information not only makes important decisions about teacher candidates' competence easier, it makes it possible for faculty members to do a better job preparing teachers. Illustrations of their students' actual work in practica and courses can help faculty members determine where preservice teacher's areas of strength and weakness exist. This information enables them to make more appropriate and pointed recommendations for improvement.

## Digital Teaching Portfolios Promote Continuity Throughout Teacher Preparation Programs

Implementing teaching portfolios in professional preparation programs can create continuity among the various and often disparate program components experienced by teacher certification candidates. Digital teaching portfolios provide an arena for demonstrating candidates' development resulting from experiences in coursework, practica, and seminars. When preparing digital teaching portfolios, candidates have opportunities to reflect on what they learned in each individual experience and then consider how the reflection of this learning can be organized around common themes. Through this process, students gain a better understanding of the various components of their professional preparation. Developing a portfolio around a common theme or standards encourages students to make connections between what they learned in various experiences.

## Digital Teaching Portfolios Help Build Community in Teacher Preparation Programs

Increased requirements set forth by teacher candidates and national and state organizations have resulted in an increased workload for teacher preparation program faculty. In many cases, increased requirements have resulted in additional teaching for faculty. Often, these faculty are so busy incorporating new standards that they have little time to communicate with colleagues. Faculty members who coordinate with one another in activities revolving around digital teaching portfolio development have an avenue for communication about topics of mutual concern. By sharing ideas and goals for students' portfolios, they might better determine how to combine the expectations they have for their students and work better as a team.

## SUMMARY

In this chapter, we described how others, besides teachers, may benefit from portfolios. Principals benefit from digital teaching portfolios because portfolios help them to evaluate teachers' and teacher candidates' teaching and technical competence. School districts in which teachers create digital teaching portfolios benefit because they employ teachers who understand authentic assessment, know how the portfolio process benefits students, can chart their own professional growth, and possess technical skills that might be used to enhance teaching and learning. In addition, we explained ways that teacher preparation programs might benefit from incorporating the development of digital teaching portfolios in their certification programs. Such efforts might help organizations preparing teachers deal with accountability, better prepare graduates, and increase collegiality among faculty members.

## CHECK YOUR UNDERSTANDING

1. In what ways can principals benefit from digital teaching portfolios?
2. How can school districts benefit from teachers creating digital teaching portfolios?
3. How can teacher preparation programs benefit from preservice teacher education students creating digital teaching portfolios? How can faculty members benefit?

# The Digital Teaching Portfolio Process

In Paul Masson wine commercials from the 1970s, Orson Welles used to say, "We will sell no wine before its time." Just as it takes time to plant seeds, cultivate their growth, and turn the grapes into wine that all might enjoy, it takes time, reflection, and organization to develop a quality portfolio. Before you begin developing your digital teaching portfolio, it is a good idea to understand the scope of the digital teaching portfolio development process. We recommend you read all of Part two before you begin developing your portfolio. Doing so will provide you with a holistic view of the process.

There is no one right way to create a portfolio, just as there is no one right way to blend and age a critically acclaimed wine. However, our experiences witnessing many teachers create digital teaching portfolios have taught us that there are more and less effective approaches! To save yourself time later and to enhance your portfolio experience, we suggest that you try the activities we present in the following chapters. The teachers with whom we have worked have used and enjoyed them. We believe that you will benefit too.

There are five basic stages in the development of a digital teaching portfolio. Each of these stages consists of several distinct processes, or steps. The five basic stages of the digital teaching portfolio process are:

1. **Planning the digital teaching portfolio.** In this stage, you will focus the goals of your portfolio and frame its objectives.
2. **Considering digital teaching portfolio contents.** In this stage, you will collect, select, and reflect on the materials you will include in your portfolio.
3. **Designing the digital teaching portfolio.** In this stage, you will organize your materials and assemble them into digital pieces that make up your portfolio.
4. **Evaluating the digital teaching portfolio.** In this stage, you will conduct formative evaluation to improve your portfolio-in-progress and summative evaluation to determine its quality.
5. **Publishing the digital teaching portfolio.** In this stage, you perform the necessary activities to present your portfolio materials in a format that others can view.

One important point we would like to stress is that the process of creating a digital teaching portfolio is recursive. In other words, it is not necessarily one that must progress in a linear, sequential way. Our presentation of the digital teaching portfolio development process is sequential and linear because we are communicating it in a book—a medium that confines us to a linear, sequential presentation of information. However, the five stages and steps that are part of each stage do not have to be performed in this way. Both the stages and steps may be performed in different sequences. For example, a teacher might begin by focusing her digital teaching portfolio and then collecting materials related to the focus or he or she might begin by collecting materials and then developing a focus based on these materials. Progression through the various processes does not have to be exclusive. A teacher might work on more than one step at a time. The teacher also might revisit some steps once they have been completed.

Another important point is that the creation of a digital teaching portfolio is a reflective process as well as a recursive one. The formal and informal reflection you will do while creating your portfolio benefits both you and those who will view your portfolio. The writing of formal reflections will facilitate your analysis, synthesis, and evaluation of your work. These analyses also will help your audience better understand the decisions, considerations, and accommodations you have made in the portfolio development process.

We suggest that you try the digital teaching portfolio development process as presented in the next few chapters. However, feel free to deviate from it if it does not work for you. Remember that it is important to experience all of the stages in the portfolio development process at some point. The stages and processes also should be repeated and revisited as you grow as a professional. Just like a teacher's work, a digital teaching portfolio is never done!

# Planning Your Digital Teaching Portfolio

## five

The first stage of the digital teaching portfolio development process involves two different processes that will help you plan your portfolio. In this stage, you will make decisions about the purpose of your digital teaching portfolio and its intended audience. We call this process "focusing." When planning, you also will make decisions that will help you create continuity among the various components of your digital teaching portfolio. Because this process involves fitting various pieces together, we call it "framing." Also you will learn to craft an educational philosophy statement that should demonstrate your chosen framework.

## Focusing Your Digital Teaching Portfolio

Focusing your portfolio involves identifying the purpose(s) for and intended audience of your portfolio. Because the decisions you make at this stage dramatically influence your work in future stages and steps, we suggest that you work carefully through the focusing process.

With so many good reasons for creating a digital teaching portfolio, you may wonder where to begin. We suggest you start by examining your objectives for creating a portfolio in the first place. Are you creating a portfolio to get a job or to keep one? Are you creating it to earn or renew your teaching certification? Are you creating it to demonstrate or model the portfolio process for your students? Maybe you are just creating a portfolio for fun or to help yourself organize your professional credentials.

Regardless of your answer, knowing your motivation for creating a digital teaching portfolio will help you determine its intended audience. There are many groups for whom you might create your portfolio, and it is likely that more than one group will view it. However, it helps to have one target group in mind, whether it be other teachers, your students, administrators, teacher education professors, or state certification officers. Eventually, you may want to find out information about this group so that you can customize your portfolio to meet its needs and interests. A portfolio created for your students will be very different from one created for state certification officers.

Activities 5.1 and 5.2 will help you focus your digital teaching portfolio. In Activity 5.1, you will define the purpose and audience of your portfolio. In Activity 5.2, you will communicate this awareness of purpose and audience by writing a rationale statement. The rationale statement will eventually become a part of your portfolio, communicating to all who view it your intentions for your display of professional work. During the process of writing this rationale, you may learn more about what you hope to gain from the portfolio development process.

## Activity 5.1

### DEFINING YOUR DIGITAL TEACHING PORTFOLIO'S PURPOSE AND AUDIENCE

To help define the purpose and audience of your portfolio, answer the following questions:

1. Why am I creating this portfolio in the first place?
2. What kind of portfolio do I want to create (working, presentation)?
3. Who am I creating the portfolio for (principal, professor, self, licensure board)?
4. What are my goals (short- and long-term) for creating a digital teaching portfolio?

## Activity 5.2

### DEVELOPING YOUR RATIONALE

1. Read the rationale statement (page 43) that was included in a preservice teacher's digital teaching portfolio and consider the following questions as you read:
   - What was the teacher's purpose for creating the portfolio?
   - What does it reveal about the teacher as an educator?

- What are the teacher's future plans for the portfolio?
- Do you believe it is important to include a rationale/purpose statement in your portfolio? Why or why not?
- For whom has the teacher written the rationale (self, principals, peers)?

### Preservice Teacher's Rationale

The purpose of my teaching portfolio is three-fold. First, I would like to use this portfolio to document my teaching experience by including lesson plans, individualized instruction, academic and behavioral interventions, and assessments. Second, I hope that this teaching portfolio will reveal who I am as an educator and an individual. As I state in my Teaching Philosophy, my approach to education is student-centered, accommodating, dynamic, and personalized. Third, I look forward to using this teaching portfolio as a tool to guide my reflection and professional growth. I consider my teaching portfolio to be a professional work in progress, which I will use to evaluate and enhance my teaching efforts throughout my career as an educator.

I pursued an electronic portfolio to further my competency in technology. This endeavor serves to illustrate my dedication to staying abreast of technology and implementing it in my classroom as much as possible. Computers are the future. I realize that for my students to be prepared for the future, I must be skilled in a variety of computer resources.

2. Write a rationale statement (using any word processing program) for your portfolio. Save the file in rich text format (RTF). Also feel free to save it in HTML format if you prefer. Good names for this file would be "rationale1_0.rtf" or "rationale1_0.html," depending on the format in which it is saved.

# Framing Your Digital Teaching Portfolio

Another process that is helpful in planning your digital teaching portfolio is the development of a framework for the presentation of your work. During this step, you will set up structures that will enable you to create continuity among the various components of your portfolio. The framing of your portfolio will fit the various pieces together. There are many creative ways to frame your portfolio.

It is likely that you have had experiences designing curriculum units. Consider for a moment that creating your digital teaching portfolio is similar to designing a curriculum unit. Just as a good unit has continuity, so does a good portfolio. In a unit, continuity is created through the continual reflection of a certain set of common goals or objectives. Portfolios with continuity do the same. This does not mean that they are rigid, stuffy, or boring. It simply means that portfolios are "glued" together with a central theme or underlying framework.

Continuity in a digital teaching portfolio might be communicated through a set of recurring ideas, values, or metaphors. For example, a teacher who believes that children are unique and individual might choose to organize her portfolio so that it communicates these principles. Her philosophy of education, in which she states this belief, could be the portfolio's focal point. She believes she might create and repeat a graphic design that extends this belief. Because children and snowflakes are alike in that no two are exactly alike, she might create a graphic on the computer using snowflakes in the design and repeat it throughout her work. In addition, she might present her professional knowledge of students' individual differences by including books she has read to develop her understanding of students' learning styles or learning contracts she has created with individual students.

Using a pattern to illustrate a teacher's professional growth also might create continuity in a digital teaching portfolio. For example, a beginning teacher who wants to communicate his professional growth during his first year of teaching might organize his work around a timeline. Instead of a table of contents, he might ask viewers to examine his professional growth by looking at a picture of a timeline. For each tick in the timeline over the first nine months of his new position, he could attach a dated piece of work and a reflection of why this work is important in his professional growth. Over time, this time-oriented representation of his efforts might prove to be an excellent tool with which to chart his future growth and development.

In the sections that follow, we suggest three different strategies for framing your digital teaching portfolio. You will learn about approaches for framing your portfolio around standards, themes, and questions. Each approach has proven to be an effective way to communicate continuity in portfolios. Keep in mind that these suggestions are not intended to limit your creativity.

## Framing Your Digital Teaching Portfolio Around Standards

As discussed in Chapter 2, several organizations promote the use of portfolios as a means of demonstrating and evaluating teachers' professional competence. Standards have been developed to evaluate teachers. Teachers might use these standards to consider ways they demonstrate competence.

Creating a portfolio that communicates your competence framed around a set of national standards is useful for at least two reasons. First, because national standards represent the collective effort of many knowledgeable education professionals who have defined indicators of good teaching, we can be ensured that they are pretty accurate benchmarks for measuring teaching competence. Teachers who design their digital teaching portfolios in ways that are responsive to standards can identify areas where their practice measures up to standards and areas in which they do not. This might provide useful information for reflection and result in the charting of goals for professional growth. Framing a portfolio around standards can help teachers examine their knowledge and skills and allow them to see how their professional practice stacks up to what leaders in the education field consider good teaching. Second, because standards are nationally recognized, a portfolio designed around such standards has the advantage of being something that has meaning to people in various communities (i.e., geographic, academic, etc.). For example, a portfolio that is designed around the ISTE's technology standards for teachers (see http://cnets.iste.org) holds the same clout in Alabama as in Wyoming.

So, which standards should you choose? If you are a teacher candidate, you may wish to organize your digital teaching portfolio around standards developed by your school of education, state board of education, or INTASC (Darling-Hammond 1992) (see http://www.ccsso.org/intascst.html). Experienced inservice teachers might choose standards provided by the state licensure board or the NBPTS (see http://www.nbpts.org).

Several Web sites provide links to different standards. Wappingers Central School District's "Developing Educational Standards" site provides teachers with links to professional standards produced by various groups for many areas of professional competence (http://edStandards.org/Standards.html). Also, two other Web sites offer K–12 standards that teachers may be interested in examining:

- Education World's Web site, "U.S. Education Standards," available at http://www.education-world.com/standards/national/index.shtml
- Mid-continent Research for Education and Learning's "Standards" site (McREL), available at http://www.mcrel.org/standards/index.asp.

Activity 5.3 is intended to help you frame your digital teaching portfolio around a set of standards. The standards will form the foundation for the entire portfolio. All items within the portfolio should help demonstrate and illustrate your competence related to the standards.

## Activity 5.3

### FRAMING YOUR DIGITAL TEACHING PORTFOLIO AROUND STANDARDS

1. Review the standards you think are most appropriate for your situation (e.g., the INTASC or NBPTS standards).
2. Create a chart (see Table 5.1 for an example of one based on the INTASC standards) to "plot" artifacts that address the standards (one artifact can address more than one standard).
3. Select artifacts that demonstrate competence in the standards (see Chapter 6 for information on how to select artifacts for your digital teaching portfolio).
4. Determine a plan for how you will later include artifacts for standards that have not been addressed.

### TABLE 5.1

#### Sample Chart to Log INTASC Principles Addressed

| INTASC Principles | Artifact |
|---|---|
| **Principle #1:** The teacher understands the central concepts, tools of inquiry, and structures of the discipline(s) he or she teaches and can create learning experiences that make these aspects of subject matter meaningful for students. | Letter of reference |
| **Principle #2:** The teacher understands how children learn and develop and can provide learning opportunities that support their intellectual, social, and personal development. | Recycling unit<br>Educational philosophy statement<br>Case study |

| | |
|---|---|
| **Principle #3:** The teacher understands how students differ in their approaches to learning and creates instructional opportunities that are adapted to diverse learners. | Educational philosophy statement<br>Video of me teaching |
| **Principle #4:** The teacher understands and uses a variety of instructional strategies to encourage students' development of critical thinking, problem solving, and performance skills. | Educational philosophy statement<br>Video of me teaching |
| **Principle #5:** The teacher uses an understanding of individual and group motivation and behavior to create a learning environment that encourages positive social interaction, active engagement in learning, and self-motivation. | Educational philosophy statement<br>Clinical faculty or principal observation |
| **Principle #6:** The teacher uses knowledge of effective verbal, non-verbal, and media communication techniques to foster active inquiry, collaboration, and supportive interaction in the classroom. | Peer observation |
| **Principle #7:** The teacher plans instruction based upon knowledge of subject matter, students, the community, and curriculum goals. | Immigration unit |
| **Principle #8:** The teacher understands and uses formal and informal assessment strategies to evaluate and ensure the continuous intellectual, social, and physical development of the learner. | Assessment plans<br>Individual Education Plan (IEP) |
| **Principle #9:** The teacher is a reflective practitioner who continually evaluates the effects of his/her choices and actions on others (students, parents, and other professionals in the learning community) and who actively seeks out opportunities to grow professionally. | Reflective statements in portfolio<br>Sample journal entries from student teaching<br>Professional development plan (long- and short-term goals) |
| **Principle #10:** The teacher fosters relationships with school colleagues, parents, and agencies in the larger community to support students' learning and well-being. | Newsletters to parents<br>Parent workshops |

## Framing Your Digital Teaching Portfolio Around a Theme

Another way to organize your digital teaching portfolio is around a theme. Some teachers feel that the method used to demonstrate their competence is a further illustration of their artistry as a teacher. For these teachers, the organization of their portfolio will express their talent and creativity just as much as the artifacts contained within it do. One rewarding way to organize a portfolio is to develop it around a common theme and then design the portfolio so that the theme is reflected in as many ways as possible.

For example, one teacher we know had a lifelong interest in trees. She loved to climb them as a child, rake their leaves as a teenager, and photograph them as an adult. When she was presented with the task of creating her digital teaching portfolio the same day that tree surgeons came to take down a tree in her backyard, this teacher got a creative idea—she would organize her entire portfolio around trees. First, she created a philosophy of education that expressed her beliefs about education using several different quotations about trees. One was a quote by Alexander

Pope: "As the tree is bent, so the tree's inclined." The teacher then packed her digital teaching portfolio full of artifacts that illustrated her growth throughout her career. Each item was dated and viewers linked to each item by clicking on the cross section of a tree trunk that had various growth circles highlighted. She included an original thematic unit she had created about trees and recycling and filled the portfolio with photographs that she had taken of different trees. After reviewing this portfolio, few could doubt the teacher's professional competence, her ability to package ideas for easy understanding, or her skill as a storyteller!

Creating a portfolio around a theme can be a rewarding and creative experience. Complete Activity 5.4 to develop your digital teaching portfolio around a theme.

---

### Activity 5.4

#### DEVELOPING YOUR DIGITAL TEACHING PORTFOLIO AROUND A THEME

To develop your digital teaching portfolio around a theme, ask yourself the following questions:

1. Is there any metaphor, idea, or image that recurs in my life or sums up who I am as a teacher?
2. How could I demonstrate my professional talents by illustrating them through this theme?
3. What artifacts might I include to reflect this theme?
4. How might I use the help of others to make sure that my theme is consistent and comprehensible?

---

## Framing Your Digital Teaching Portfolio Around a Question

You also can frame your portfolio around a question. When a portfolio is created this way, the question is formed first and then all artifacts emanate from the question and its answer. Basing a digital teaching portfolio around a question makes the portfolio the center of self-inquiry and reflection. Viewing a portfolio designed this way allows the viewer to explore various facets of a teacher's professionalism and catch a glimpse of the teacher's thinking processes.

Here we provide some questions that have been used to frame the portfolios of teachers with whom we have worked. Although you might use these questions as the basis for your portfolio, it is better for you, the *teacher*, to develop your own guiding question for your portfolio. Some examples of portfolio questions are:

- How do I develop and implement a learning environment based on constructivist principles?
- How can I help students become good problem solvers?
- How do I provide activities that incorporate multiple intelligences?
- How can I help students conduct research and problem-solve like real scientists?

Grant and Huebner (1998, pp. 156–171) provide some guidelines for developing a powerful question. These guidelines suggest that a good question be:

- **Practice-based.** It should come from a problem or experience that occurred in the classroom.
- **Professionally relevant.** It should revolve around something that is of concern or great interest to the teacher candidate or inservice teacher.
- **Significant.** The question should be important enough to be able to build a portfolio around it.
- **Honest.** The preservice or inservice teacher should not have any bias or preconceived ideas about the question.
- **Precisely stated.** The question should be tied to pedagogical issues in a succinct, clear manner.

Keep in mind that the development of a question is a process. Crafting a good question, one that is important and can be answered with examples of your work as a professional, is difficult. You will not come up with a good question overnight. You may need to revise the question multiple times, even after the portfolio development process has begun. Activity 5.5 outlines some strategies for developing a digital teaching portfolio question.

## Activity 5.5

### DEVELOPING A DIGITAL TEACHING PORTFOLIO QUESTION

To develop your digital teaching portfolio question, do the following:

1. Brainstorm some questions that you might like to use for the basis of your portfolio.
2. For each question you develop, review and examine how your question stacks up to Grant and Huebner's (1998) guidelines for developing a powerful question.
3. Ask someone to read your questions and provide feedback.
4. Revise, revise, and revise the question until you are satisfied. You may even want to collect, select, and reflect on some artifacts that might support the question to see if it meets Grant and Huebner's criteria.

# Developing Your Educational Philosophy Statement

An important component of any digital teaching portfolio is the educational (or teaching) philosophy statement. If you have not already done so, we recommend you develop or fine-tune your *educational philosophy statement* at this stage of the digital teaching portfolio development process. We have included it in this stage because the educational philosophy statement also can be centered on standards, themes, or a question. Moreover, having this statement fleshed out will likely help you a great deal in selecting your artifacts.

The educational philosophy statement is a description of your beliefs about teaching and learning. (Figure 5.1 is an example of a teacher's educational philosophy) Although it may seem like a simple task, developing your educational philosophy statement can be one of the most difficult tasks you will encounter during the entire digital teaching portfolio development process. Your philosophy may start or end with a quote, such as William Butler Yeat's quote: "Education is not the filling of a pail, but the lighting of a fire." You may also include concrete examples of your beliefs about teaching and learning or describe your approaches to teaching.

**FIGURE 5.1**  Sample Educational Philosophy Statement

### The Importance of Education: El Saber es el Poder

My educational philosophy is driven by the belief that "el saber es el poder." In English, the phrase literally means "knowledge is the ability to. . . ." I like to say it means knowledge is power, strength, and possibility. It empowers one with the ability to accomplish things.

Education has always been very important to me, and it has always been an integral part of my life. I see myself as a lifelong learner who will always be learning through research, experience, and interaction with others. One reason that I desire to be a teacher is that I want to share what I have learned with children, but also look forward to learning even more from my students.

One of my undergraduate professors once told me that all he desired, all that he hoped for, was to help his students learn. He explained his desire by asking me to imagine myself standing on his shoulders and seeing a little further into the horizon, and thus seeing beyond his scope of vision. I hope to achieve the same goal: to help my students see at a greater distance into the horizon than I can see.

### Perspective on Teaching

Teaching is extremely challenging. Before I had the responsibility of teaching a class of seven-year-old second graders, I had a very naive view of how much energy, time, and planning would be involved. It was surprising to me how complex, demanding, and rewarding teaching could be. Words cannot express the gratification in successfully teaching a child to read, helping a parent understand his/her child's academic difficulties, and motivating a teacher to use technology in his/her instruction.

Since my first few days in the classroom, I have spent much time reflecting on what my perspective of good teaching is, recollecting my impressions of teachers/professors (throughout my many years of studies), mentors, colleagues, and most important, my first teachers, my parents. I also have critically analyzed my own teaching strengths, weaknesses, and style, which has inspired me to experiment with new strategies and to consult with more experienced teachers for their advice.

For me, a teacher is one who is respectful, understanding, approachable, and supportive. The way I interact with students demonstrates my respect for them. For example, I never say anything derogatory to them or use them (or any of their work) as a poor example. I illustrate understanding by listening to their needs, even if I am unable to comply. Because I treat students with respect and understanding, I am approachable; students often ask for additional help and thank me for making them feel comfortable and not intimidated for asking questions. When I work with students, I am supportive of their ideas and desires. For instance, once a student wanted to work on a project that I thought would be difficult for him. Rather than not approve the topic, I helped him find and organize the resources necessary to complete the project successfully. If anything, I would hope that my past, present, and future students perceive me to have these qualities, too.

### Perspective on Learning

*Learning is a lifelong process.* I find it difficult to divide any experience from learning, and I do not think that any day passes that I do not learn something. Life is experience, and experience is learning.

*We learn by example.* When I taught second grade, my students had difficulty understanding how to write a simple paragraph. I quickly learned the power of providing examples for them by writing an example on chart paper and explaining what I was thinking as I wrote. Too often, teachers assume that students have learned the basics (or even more complex topics).

*We learn by doing.* Children learn to read by reading, people learn to use computers by using them. In essence, we internalize new experiences by performing those exact tasks. This reminds me of an ancient Chinese proverb:

> Tell me, I forget.
> Show me, I remember.
> Involve me, I understand.

*We learn by creating our own meaning.* There are so many factors, including our own past experiences, that influence our learning. No matter how we attempt to assess student learning or how much we impose our ideas upon students, they will create their own meaning and understanding of the material. Learning is situated in the past and present interactions that the students have experienced, over which instructors have no control.

*We learn through discovery.* Especially in regards to using new technologies, I find that we learn best through exploration and by trying new things. It would be easy (and boring) for me to explain to students step-by-step how to create a database, but it is more fun and interesting for them to discover on their own how to create one (with some guidance).

*We learn from our mistakes.* Some of my best learning experiences were gleaned from my mistakes. In several cases, I learned that a particular strategy was not effective, and should not be used again; in others, I learned that it should be repeated.

### Perspective on Teaching and Instructional Technology

In today's Information Age, I believe it is imperative for teachers at all academic levels to employ technology in their instruction, in particular because it is so prevalent in our society. There is not one facet of life that is not tied to technology in some way. However, I also believe it is important to utilize technology in meaningful ways and with purpose. Simply using technology for technology's sake defeats the purpose. Further, technology should be used to make things easier and more efficient, not to make things more complicated.

Technological literacy is also vital, and will become increasingly important as we become more and more dependent on technology. Not only will students need to understand how to use technology as tools, they will also need to know how to solve problems using these tools.

Technology refers to any type of tool that may be used for instructional purposes, which includes, but is not limited to, books, cameras, calculators, compasses, computer hardware and software, digital media, microscopes, video, and the Web. I do not promote the use of technology for such activities as "drill and practice" or only word processing. My idea of the effective use of technology entails enriching ways where students examine and use technology to demonstrate their knowledge of subject areas. Oftentimes, technology is taught in isolation of subject areas, rather than integrated across the curriculum.

There is no magic formula for writing your educational philosophy statement. Just try writing your honest thoughts using a computer word processing program. Try to make it between 300 to 400 words. You should strive for a serious but not pompous tone, conveying your thoughts with clarity as well as with perfect spelling, punctuation, and grammar. (This is even more important when you make your portfolio available on the World Wide Web, because anyone can read it, you will want to be sure to demonstrate skills appropriate for a person modeling such proficiency to children!) It may help to consider a school administrator as your audience. Use a word processing program to write an educational statement that will let a person know where you stand in regard to important educational theories and practices. Have a colleague or a school parent you trust review your educational philosophy statement and provide feedback.

Use the questions in Figure 5.2 to help you think about your beliefs regarding education. Spend some time thinking about each one in some depth. It is not necessary to respond to each of these questions in your written philosophy. You also may decide to comment on additional issues as well.

Save your educational philosophy statement in RTF or HTML. Also do not forget to run a spell check. Save the file with an appropriate name and version (e.g., philosophy_2_0.rtf), log the file name in a database or chart to help you determine which standards(s) it addresses (if you have one), and make at least one extra copy of the file elsewhere (see Chapter 10 for places where you might consider backing up your work).

FIGURE 5.2   Questions for Developing an Educational Philosophy Statement

1. In your opinion, what are the broad goals of education? How can they best be met?
2. What are your hopes for each of your (present/future) students? What do you want them to achieve, accomplish, learn, feel, etc.?
3. What kind of knowledge and skills do you believe are most important for students, and how should they gain that knowledge and those skills? What will be your role in that process?
4. What do you believe about the learning process? How does learning take place?
5. How will your beliefs influence your teaching?
6. Will you consciously promote certain values in your classroom? If so, which values will you choose? Why? If not, why not?
7. What kind of environment do you hope to create in your classroom? How does this relate to your basic beliefs about students and learning?
8. What kind of feedback will you offer your students as they work? How will you use praise, rewards, punishment, etc.? What kind of assessment will you use to be sure that students have met objectives?
9. How do you view students as learners?
10. What is your teaching style?
11. What strategies do you use when teaching?
12. Why do you teach the way you teach?

## SUMMARY

In this chapter, we explained that focusing and framing your digital teaching portfolio during the planning stage is important because decisions made in this stage influence future stages and processes. You learned that focusing a portfolio involves deciding on the purpose of the portfolio and its intended audience. Identification of the portfolio's purpose is important so that it will be clear to the person reviewing the portfolio. Recognition of the primary audience is important so that the needs of the audience are addressed in the design and presentation of materials. You also learned that framing a digital teaching portfolio involves making decisions about how continuity will be created among materials included in the portfolio. Various strategies for framing portfolios exist. They include designing a portfolio so that it (1) is responsive to standards, (2) revolves around a theme, or (3) emanates from a question. In addition, we discussed the crafting of an educational philosophy statement.

## CHECK YOUR UNDERSTANDING

1. What should you consider when developing the focus of your digital teaching portfolio?
2. What are some ways in which you might frame your digital teaching portfolio?
3. How is the focusing and framing process similar to designing lesson plans?
4. Why is it important to focus and frame your digital teaching portfolio?

# Considering
# Digital Teaching
# Portfolio Materials

The steps you perform in this stage of the digital teaching portfolio development process are the same steps you perform when creating a curriculum unit. You *collect* the resources you wish to consider for inclusion, *select* from the array of artifacts and resources available based on some kind of criteria or purpose, and *reflect* on how these pieces fit together to best communicate your intended goals. Before we explain how you will collect, select, and reflect on portfolio content, we describe some of the resources, often called artifacts, that you may wish to include in your portfolio.

## What Are the Ingredients of Your Digital Teaching Portfolio?

The resources you include in your digital teaching portfolio can be classified into two basic categories: artifacts and supporting documentation. Artifacts are the elements critical to the focus and framework of your portfolio. They are the resources that demonstrate your professional knowledge and competence. Resources classified as supporting documentation do not fall into the artifact category. They are resources that are meaningful because they communicate other important information about you as a person when you are not teaching and about your portfolio, they also include materials that explain your portfolio organization, but are not critical to the focus and frame of the actual portfolio. These resources might include personal information, the rationale statement, and a table of contents.

## Artifacts

An artifact is "tangible evidence that indicates the attainment of knowledge and skills and the ability to apply understandings to complex tasks" (Campbell, Melenyzer, Nettles, and Wyman, 2000 p. 147). Résumés, lesson plans, educational philosophy statements, and classroom management plans are all considered tangible evidence of teachers' knowledge. Most teachers should have little trouble locating artifacts that demonstrate their teaching competence and knowledge, especially if they are organized! Table 6.1 provides a listing of the professional artifacts teachers might decide to include in a digital teaching portfolio. For a comprehensive listing of portfolio artifact definitions, see Appendix B of Campbell, Melenyzer, Nettles, and Wyman (2000).

## Supporting Documentation

You may wonder why you would want to include items in your digital teaching portfolio that are not artifacts. There are two reasons. First, some of these items help to organize and present the contents of your portfolio to others. Supporting documentation ties the portfolio together. A table of contents does not present information about a teacher's knowledge and competence, but it does help the viewer access this information. The rationale statement may not communicate any critical information about a teacher's professionalism, but it will communicate the reasons the teacher chose to demonstrate her professionalism in a portfolio. Second, items that fall in the supporting documentation category help communicate important personal information about the teacher as a person. This supporting documentation makes a portfolio more interesting.

We are sure many of you have bumped into your students outside of your classrooms at checkout counters, in restaurants, and at the public library. For many students, it was probably hard for them to imagine that their teacher is a real person who does *not* live at school (although we are sure that many days it seems that way). Providing personal information, such as information about your family, hobbies, and interests, can help students and others realize that you are a real person with a real family with, believe it or not, a life outside of teaching! Inclusion of such information also may offer principals, parents, and teacher education professors with

TABLE 6.1

## Types of Professional Artifacts

| Theory and Beliefs | Education and Experience | Curriculum, Planning, and Management | Student Assessment | Communication |
|---|---|---|---|---|
| ■ Educational philosophy statement<br>■ Goals (short- and long-term)<br>■ Mission statement<br>■ Reflective statements<br>■ Research papers<br>■ Case studies<br>■ Professional development plan<br>■ Description of learning environment<br>■ Journal entries | ■ Résumé<br>■ Transcripts<br>■ Awards, grants, and honors<br>■ References or recommendations<br>■ Teaching evaluations<br>■ Classroom observations<br>■ Professional development records (evaluations and awards)<br>■ List of Web sites that are influential in growth and development<br>■ Record of books read<br>■ Special skills or knowledge (such as ability to use/teach with certain software programs<br>■ Description of workshops, training, for-credit courses taken<br>■ Observations by others (peers, master teacher, principal) | ■ Long-term plans or themes for the year<br>■ Units<br>■ Lesson plans<br>■ WebQuests<br>■ Student work samples<br>■ Videos<br>■ Photographs<br>■ Seating chart<br>■ Classroom management plan<br>■ Classroom rules<br>■ Daily schedule<br>■ Course Web site | ■ Anecdotal records of student progress<br>■ Student evaluation plans<br>■ Individual educational plans (IEP) for students<br>■ Evaluations of student work<br>■ Rubrics<br>■ Student portfolios<br>■ Student journal entries | ■ Letters to and from students/parents<br>■ Newsletters<br>■ Memos<br>■ Parent-teacher conferences (notes, questions) |

information highlighting your accomplishments outside the classroom. Inclusion of personal information in your portfolio helps to show that you are well-rounded, part of a community, and interesting.

However, we do have some words of caution about sharing your personal information. Ask yourself how much information you want to share about yourself or those close to you. In this day and age, we must be careful about what and how much we disclose about others and ourselves (Digital Teaching Portfolio Commandment #6: Pay heed to legal and security concerns, see Chapter 10).

The rest of this section provides descriptions of some of the supporting documentation you might consider including in your digital teaching portfolio. However, our list of items is not exhaustive. We are sure you can think of many other items that could be included in your portfolio.

**AUTHORSHIP STATEMENT.**   The authorship statement is a statement communicating who is responsible for the creation of the various materials contained in the digital teaching portfolio and expressing the authenticity of the materials. During a conference presentation on digital teaching portfolios, a gentleman in the audience inquired about the authenticity of materials included in a portfolio we were demonstrating and wanted to know whether there was any guarantee that the portfolios created by teachers reflected work that they had created. This gentleman's concern about authorship and authenticity made us realize that it is a good idea to include a statement in a portfolio that explains that the portfolio is the original work of the teacher, unless otherwise noted. A simple authorship statement to this effect could say: "This digital teaching portfolio contains my original work, unless otherwise noted."

**CREDITS.**   The credits acknowledge various individuals who have contributed to your professionalism as a teacher today or who will contribute to the great teacher you will someday become. In this section, you may wish to recognize people who have coached you along the way (such as your critical friends). The credits also might give you a place to express gratitude to those who were helpful or perhaps even "saviors" (maybe the technology coordinator at your school) in helping you accomplish the monumental task of creating your digital teaching portfolio.

**DEDICATION.**   The dedication provides portfolio creators with a place to recognize individuals who are important to them.

**PERMISSION STATEMENT.**   The permission statement demonstrates that you have received permission to present the work of others in your digital teaching portfolio. If you present the work of more than one other individual, this statement references all others' work and photos. Here is a sample permission statement: "I have received written permission from colleagues, students (and their parents), and anyone else whose work or images I have chosen to showcase in my Web-based digital teaching portfolio. The names of these individuals have been shortened, changed, or deleted to protect their identity." Consent forms for students (and their parents) and colleagues are available in Appendix C. See Chapter 10 for more information about permissions.

**RATIONALE STATEMENT.**   The rationale statement describes your motivation and the purpose for displaying your selected work in a portfolio. The rationale statement is often a nice way to introduce your digital teaching portfolio, and it is appropriately placed at the top of the table of contents. (See Activity 5.2 in Chapter 5 for an example of a rationale statement written by a teacher candidate.)

**TABLE OF CONTENTS.** The table of contents communicates the organization of your digital teaching portfolio and describes its content. Often, the table of contents serves as the navigation scheme linking the different parts of your digital teaching portfolio. (See Figure 7.1 for an example of a table of contents, or index page, for a portfolio).

# Collecting Digital Teaching Portfolio Content

The process of collecting materials for possible inclusion in your digital teaching portfolio can be a very tedious and nerve-wracking one if you are not organized. And, let's face it, not all of us are as organized as we would like to be. Whatever kind of pack rat you are, you will first want to locate as many artifacts as possible. Although the eventual focus of your collection will be on quality, identifying the very best items that you may include, at this time you want to focus on quantity, collecting a large group of items to select from. The more items you have to choose from, the more choices you will have in the selection process. Every choice you make about materials will lead to your professional growth, so leave no stone unturned!

Also, remember to collect materials you would consider to be works-in-progress, even items that are incomplete. Such artifacts might provide some of the most interesting information about your development as a teacher. For example, imagine that one day you worked very hard to develop a lesson on the addition of double-digit numbers. Days before you finished planning the lesson, your mentor teacher shared a great hands-on lesson for teaching the same topic. As a result, you realized that the approach you were taking to teach the topic was way off, and you planned on deleting the lesson from your computer. However, the incomplete lesson, as bad as you perceived it to be, might be just the item you want to include because it shows how you can learn from your experiences, apply new approaches, and recognize your weaknesses! So, we recommend you collect as many items as possible to consider for inclusion in your portfolio.

Based on our work with teachers, we believe that there are certain items that *every* digital teaching portfolio should include. These include a rationale statement and an educational philosophy statement, among other items. We explain in detail how to create these statements in activities tied to Chapter 5. If you have not created these statements, we urge you to consider creating them now. If you have already created these statements, collect them and save them in one place, such as a file folder (a physical one in a filing cabinet) *and* a computer file titled "portfolio."

Use Activity 6.1 to collect items that every digital teaching portfolio should have.

## Activity 6.1

### ARTIFACTS EVERY DIGITAL TEACHING PORTFOLIO SHOULD HAVE

1. Find and check off each item as you locate it.
   - Rationale statement
   - Permission statement
   - Classroom management plan
   - Examples of student work
   - Professional development plan
   - Résumé
   - Authorship statement
   - Assessment plan
   - Educational philosophy statement
   - Lesson plans/units
   - Reflective statements
   - Table of contents
2. Create a log (using a database or word processing program) indicating the location of these items (you also may want to reference these with standards, as shown in Table 5.1.)
3. Create backup copies of these items.

# Selecting Digital Teaching Portfolio Content

If you are going through the digital teaching portfolio process sequentially as we suggest, the next step in the second stage of the process deals with selection. In this step, you will select the items that you will include in your portfolio, otherwise known as the content (e.g., artifacts and supporting documentation).

The selection of portfolio content is an important, challenging, and rewarding part of the portfolio process. It is important because the selection process will result in the identification of materials that will actually comprise your digital teaching portfolio. These materials will communicate your competence as a teacher and other dimensions of your professionalism. These materials also may influence the software you will eventually use to publish your portfolio. This step is challenging because it involves many decisions regarding what kinds of resources to include, which samples of resources to include, and how many resources to include (e.g., the number of lesson plans). These decisions take a great deal of energy and thought. Sometimes, they require you to seek the advice of others. Finally, the process is rewarding because it will enable you to review the work you have accomplished as a teacher and encourage you to reflect on it. This is indeed a valuable process.

Once you have collected your artifacts, you are ready to begin examining them to select those appropriate for inclusion in your portfolio. At this stage in the process, your energy should be redirected from quantity to *quality*. If you did your job well during the "collection" step, you will have a large number of materials to choose from in the "selection" step. If you do your job well in this step, you will select the items that best reflect your focus and fit in your framework.

You will base the selection of artifacts upon certain criteria. These criteria should relate directly to the framework of your portfolio (i.e., standards, theme, or question). For instance, if your portfolio is focused around standards, then you will develop criteria that relate to the standards. Criteria might require that artifacts: (1) reflect accomplishment of specific standards, (2) illustrate continuous instructional improvement related to standards over time, and (3) communicate accomplishment of specific standards.

For example, consider these two standards:

- **INTASC Standards Principle #7 (Teacher Candidates).** The teacher plans instruction based upon knowledge of subject matter, students, the community, and curriculum goals.
- **NBPTS Standards for Middle Childhood/Generalist (Inservice Teachers).** *Knowledge of Content and Curriculum*: Accomplished teachers draw on their knowledge of subject matter and curriculum to make sound decisions about what is important for students to learn within and across the subject areas that comprise the middle childhood curriculum.

Each of these standards deals with the role of professional knowledge in teaching and developing curriculum. A good way to demonstrate competence in each of these standards is to select lesson plans that you have written and/or taught that are tied to national or local standards for students (e.g., district-level or state standards) that demonstrate your knowledge about the curriculum and your students. These lessons may be a portion of a unit or an entire one. Later, you may want to include reflective statements describing why you chose the particular unit and how it related to your students. (We discuss how to develop reflective statements later in this chapter.) Figure 6.1 shows the introduction to a unit that was developed by a teacher candidate. This example shows how a teacher can demonstrate accomplishment of INTASC Principle #7. As shown in Figure 6.1, the teacher candidate introduces the unit with a description of the unit goals and objectives and includes links to the lessons that comprise the unit, as well as reflective statements about the lessons.

Although it is possible to include every single artifact you can think of in your digital teaching portfolio, this is neither feasible nor desirable. It is not feasible because it will take too much time and too much energy! There are several reasons why it is not desirable.

First, you do not want to subject your audience to more artifacts if reviewing fewer artifacts might accomplish your objectives just as well. If it takes too long to view your work, the audiences you most want to impress may tune out before experiencing your most important content. Think: Less is more! Second, the process that goes into selecting the best or most appropriate artifacts from a larger body of artifacts can be valuable. This process requires you to make deliberate decisions based on various criteria (e.g., Is the work my best work? Does it demonstrate growth? Does it reflect a standard?). When you compare work against certain criteria (regardless of what the criteria are), you critically consider whether the artifacts stack up to the criteria or not. In many cases, this means teachers are recognizing various significant attributes of their work and learning about their own progress. By including materials without making any decisions about them, an opportunity for important professional reflection is missed.

FIGURE 6.1 Unit Lesson Plan on Recycling

**"Reduce, Reuse, Recycle (It's Easy to Do)"**

These kindergarten science lessons, which I designed with my partner, target the Virginia Standards of Learning (SOLs) for Resources (K.10). Key concepts from the SOLs that we covered in the three lessons include "describing everyday materials that can be recycled" (**Lesson One/Direct Instruction**) and "identifying materials and objects that can be used over and over again" (**Lesson Two/Concept Attain-ment**). For our third lesson, we discussed composting, or "natural recycling," with the children—everyday materials such as kitchen and yard waste can be used over and over again by turning them into humus, or fertilizer. Because kindergartners have limited reading and writing abilities and relatively short attention spans, we constructed active lessons that included read alouds, concept sorts, and art activities. Because kindergartners also have difficulty thinking abstractly, we provided many concrete materials. Students used science process skills of observation, prediction, classification, and communication during this mini-unit.

I have included these lessons in my portfolio to show some of my earliest efforts in lesson planning. I believe that my partner and I created engaging and challenging hands-on activities for the kindergartners, and we learned much as a result of the process of planning, teaching, and reflecting.

Lesson One: Recycling      Lesson Two: Reusing

Lesson Three: Composting      Reflections

## Quantity versus Quality when Selecting Artifacts

Finally, we have one comment on how the format of *digital* teaching portfolios can influence artifact selection. In the old days when portfolios were created in hard copy, failure to select artifacts carefully resulted in the inclusion of many, many artifacts. Some traditional portfolios were very large in size or very heavy. These big, unwieldy, heavy portfolios often had to be dragged or lugged around with the aid of a special carrying bag or in some cases a forklift! Today, producing a portfolio in digital format makes it possible to include even more documents without increasing the physical size of a portfolio.

Some people believe the seemingly unlimited storage of digital devices such as CDs provide teachers a license to create bigger, more in-depth portfolios. We caution you to remember that, although having more information can be useful in illustrating your ideas, it is only useful to a point. When so much information is presented that it has the effect of being distracting, disorganized, and fails to show your best work, it can be harmful! Instead of including more artifacts for the sake of "coverage," consider fewer documents for the purpose of "uncovering" your best, most illustrative professional work. Remind yourself of the argument for quality versus quantity when selecting artifacts for your digital teaching portfolio. Finally, keep in mind that a presentation portfolio does *not* contain everything a working portfolio might contain. In Activity 6.2, we provide you with some guidelines to consider when selecting artifacts and items for inclusion in your portfolio.

## Activity 6.2

### SELECTING THE ARTIFACTS FOR YOUR DIGITAL TEACHING PORTFOLIO

Here are some guidelines for selecting artifacts:

1. Examine as many artifacts as possible (e.g., lesson plans, student work samples, etc.).
2. Determine which artifacts support the standards, theme, or question you have chosen as the foundation of your portfolio by asking yourself the following questions about *each* artifact/item:
   - Does this artifact/item meet the criteria for which I am framing my portfolio? How?
   - Is this artifact/item the best example(s) I can use for demonstrating these criteria? If so, why? If not, why not?
   - Should I include this artifact/item in my portfolio? Why or why not?
3. Create a log sheet (see Table 5.1 in Chapter 5 for a sample log sheet) of the artifacts you wish to include in your working portfolio and relate these to how they meet the standards, theme, or question you have chosen as the foundation of your portfolio. You may even want to rate the items (e.g., definitely include or maybe include).
4. Be selective. You do not have to include every lesson in a unit. You can include representative lessons.
5. Remain focused. Keep your purpose and audience in mind when selecting artifacts.

# Reflecting on Digital Teaching Portfolio Content

> A [digital teaching] portfolio without reflection is just a multimedia presentation, or a fancy electronic résumé, or a digital scrapbook (Barrett 2000).

Reflection should occur naturally throughout the *entire* digital teaching portfolio development process (and beyond). But what is reflection? Lyons (1998) defines reflection as "a drawing together of long strands of connections, the weaving together of experiences, theory, and practices into meaning for the individual teacher and a kind of construction of knowledge—a knowledge of teaching practice" (p. 106). She also explains that several definitions of reflection exist, but most have been influenced by Dewey's idea of reflection as "deliberation" and Schön's as "embodied in action" (Lyons, 1998, p. 106). We like to describe reflection as taking time to think and contemplate metacognitively about teaching practice.

Too often we teach and do and go about our day-to-day responsibilities without reflecting about why we do what we do and its impact on our students and ourselves. Most of the time we function this way because we have so many demands placed upon us on a minute-by-minute basis. This is precisely why, however you define reflection, it is also important to make time for *formal* reflection about your portfolio and to include these comments in your portfolio. Activity 6.3 is a list of questions to help you think reflectively about your artifacts.

## Activity 6.3

### QUESTIONS TO HELP YOU REFLECT ON ARTIFACTS

To help you formally reflect on the artifacts you wish to include in your digital teaching portfolio, ask yourself these questions about *each* artifact:

1. How does this artifact demonstrate competence in a particular standard or your chosen framework?
2. Why did I include this artifact? Why is it important to me?
3. What did I learn as a result of using/creating this artifact?
4. How would I do things differently as a result of the artifact?

## Writing Reflective Statements

There are several ways that you can write and organize reflective statements. You can use the questions presented in Activity 6.3 or follow guidelines that you or others have developed. Some teachers like to include reflective statements for each artifact, whereas others like to include reflections on portions of their portfolio. For National Board Certification, NBPTS (2001) requires teachers to describe, analyze, and reflect on *each* artifact they include in their portfolios.

Brown and Irby (2001) recommend the use of a specific process for structuring and developing reflective comments. The process involves five steps:

1. Select the artifact.
2. Describe the circumstances (who, what, where, when) surrounding the artifact.
3. Analyze *why* you chose this artifact and how it demonstrates competence/ knowledge of particular standards.
4. Appraise the artifact by examining and interpreting the "impact and appropriateness" (p. 32) of teacher actions and how these relate to professional knowledge.
5. Transform your practice by describing how the artifact can promote changes or growth that might improve teaching practice.

You can apply Brown and Irby's (2001) process for writing a reflective statement in Activity 6.4.

## Activity 6.4

### WRITING A REFLECTIVE STATEMENT

Instructions: Choose one artifact you plan on including in your digital teaching portfolio. Apply Brown and Irby's (2001) process for structuring and developing reflective comments by writing a reflective statement that includes the information shown here.

Date: _____

Artifact: _____

Standard: _____

_____

_____

Describe: _____

_____

_____

_____

Analyze: _____

_____

_____

_____

Appraise: _____

_____

Transform: _____

_____

_____

## SUMMARY

This chapter describes the processes involved in considering digital teaching portfolio content: collecting, selecting, and reflecting. During the collection phase, the focus is on quantity—amassing as many items as you can. The next phase, selection, entails the opposite. The goal of this phase is on choosing items that demonstrate quality, not quantity. In the final phase of this stage, formal reflection takes place. In this chapter, we provided activities that led you through this stage of the digital teaching portfolio development process. The chapter also presented a description of the types of items that may be included in the portfolio and a checklist of items that we believe every digital teaching portfolio should have.

## CHECK YOUR UNDERSTANDING

1. What are some items you might wish to include in your digital teaching portfolio?
2. What criteria will you use to select portfolio content?
3. How many items do you plan on including in your portfolio?
4. What are some items that every digital teaching portfolio should have?
5. What is the purpose of reflection in the portfolio development process?

# chapter

# Designing
# Your Digital
# Teaching Portfolio

**B**y now you have completed the first two stages of the digital teaching portfolio development process. You have planned your portfolio making decisions about the focus and framework of your portfolio. Also, you have considered portfolio content by collecting, selecting, and reflecting on portfolio content. Hopefully, you have saved and backed up your digital artifacts in folders so that they are easy to locate and transfer. If you have not backed up your work, do so now. You are now ready for the design phase of the portfolio development process. The design stage involves two distinct interrelated processes: organizing and producing.

Organizing your digital teaching portfolio involves the creation of a table of contents, the placement of artifacts into the different categories found in the table of contents, and the development of a storyboard that sketches out how artifacts will appear to the viewer. Producing the portfolio is the transformation that occurs when the storyboard and table of contents become a collection of integrated digital files. Activities in this chapter will help teachers to complete each of these processes.

# Organizing Your Digital Teaching Portfolio Contents

After you have worked through stages one (see Chapter 5) and two (see Chapter 6) of the digital teaching portfolio development process, you will have a large collection of artifacts that you want to include in your digital teaching portfolio. You must now organize these artifacts in some manner to make it easier for those viewing your digital teaching portfolio to understand them. The organization of your digital teaching portfolio's contents should be easy if you selected materials based on your focus and framework. You will simply use this framework as the basis for your organizational scheme.

There are two ways to approach the organization of your digital teaching portfolio, the low-tech way (e.g., using index cards or sticky notes) or the high-tech way (i.e., using a concept-mapping or database program). Follow whichever approach works best for you.

## Designing Your Table of Contents

An excellent way to start organizing the elements of your digital teaching portfolio is to create a table of contents. The table of contents represents the categories into which you will group the different items that will make up the portfolio. It also will serve as your navigation scheme linking the different parts of your digital teaching portfolio, especially if you use PowerPoint or Composer to create your portfolio. (For an indepth discussion of design tools, see Chapter 11.)

If you frame your digital teaching portfolio so that it is responsive to standards, the different standards will make good categories. For example, a teacher framing a portfolio around the ISTE's National Educational Technology standards might create six categories that reflect these standards: (1) Technology Operations and Concepts, (2) Planning and Designing Learning Environments and Experiences, (3) Teaching, Learning, and Curriculum, (4) Assessment and Evaluation, (5) Productivity and Professional Practice, and (6) Social, Ethical, Legal, and Human Issues. Other categories might need to be formed to include other information of a professional and personal nature.

If the framework of a digital teaching portfolio is a theme, a teacher might formulate some creative names for the categories to carry out the theme. The teacher we know who used trees as a theme (see Chapter 5) in her portfolio named her categories so that they reflected the different parts of a tree. She called the information about her professional credentials, "Roots and Professional Foundations;" information about her use of professional support people and other resources; "Trunks and Resources for Support;" information about her teaching practice, "Branches Stretching Learning," and that of her professional development, "Leaves and Signs of New Growth."

If you choose to develop your digital teaching portfolio around a question or set of questions, the questions themselves would form interesting categories. The question also might form the basis for long-term examination of your development by comparing how you address the same or different question in your portfolio over the years. A teacher exploring "How can I help students conduct research and problem-solve like real scientists?" might demonstrate this through the various categories of instructional materials, student collaboration, technology, and the like. Activity 7.1 will help you develop the categories that will form your portfolio's table of contents. An example table of contents is shown in Figure 7.1.

## Activity 7.1

### DEVELOPING YOUR TABLE OF CONTENTS

1. Revisit the frame and focus of your digital teaching portfolio.
2. Brainstorm some categories in which you might organize your portfolio items.
3. Record these categories using index cards, Inspiration, a word processing software, or a database program.  (If you use Inspiration or a word processing program that can create outlines, use the "Outline View" for recording the categories.)
4. Examine the sample table of contents (Figure 7.1).
5. Decide which categories you wish to include in your portfolio (if you have not already done so).
6. Reflect on why these categories are important to you *and* how these categories support the frame and focus of your portfolio.
7. Ask a critical friend* to review the categories and provide feedback.
8. Revise the categories based on your critical friend's feedback.
9. Begin grouping your artifacts and supporting documentation into the different categories (using index cards, Inspiration, a word processing program, or database software) by recording the items under the appropriate categories.
10. If you sorted items using a software program, save the file with a file name like "toc_1_0.html".

*A critical friend is someone who will provide you with constructive feedback about your portfolio and its contents (see Chapter 8 for more information about critical friends).

## Placing Artifacts in Different Categories

Once you have developed the table of contents, you are ready to begin grouping artifacts and supporting documentation into the different categories. In Activity 7.2, you will classify the items you chose in the selection process into the specific categories that were developed in Activity 7.1.

You can sort the items into categories using index cards or sticky notes. If these low-tech options do not appeal to you, feel free to take advantage of the graphic or

FIGURE 7.1    Sample Table of Contents

outlining features in Microsoft's products or use a concept-mapping program such as Inspiration or Kidspiration. We like to use Inspiration and Kidspiration because they are simple and have many different applications. Thirty-day trial versions of both of these software programs are available for free at http://www.inspiration.com.

## Activity 7.2

### ORGANIZING THE ITEMS IN YOUR DIGITAL TEACHING PORTFOLIO

1. Purchase a pack of 3 × 5 index cards or open a software program such as Inspiration or PowerPoint, or a word processing or database program.
2. Write a description of each resource you plan to include in your portfolio and why you plan to include it on an index card or using any of the software programs listed in the first step.
3. Start with the artifacts. For example, you might take a PowerPoint presentation you want to include and write: "PowerPoint presentation on whales created 11/2002. Demonstrates competence with district-recommended software program. Illustrates use of technology to reach students with various learning styles." Or, describe a letter you sent to parents: "Letter to parents sent 5/2002. Explains new instructional approach and policy for grading student work. Demonstrates ability to communicate effectively in writing."

4. Once you have created an index card or diagram, slide, or field for each artifact, include a brief description of all the supporting documentation you are including in your portfolio. For instance, you might write: "Rationale statement. 12/2002 Explains contents of portfolio."

5. Read through each index card or diagram, slide, or field and group the index cards, diagrams, slides, or fields (and the artifacts and supporting documentation listed on them) so that like resources are categorized together. Ideally, you will come up with five to ten major groups of items. If necessary, make subcategories for each group. For example, you might create a category called "Original Instructional Materials." In this category, you would have subgroups that might contain (a) samples of math manipulatives, (b) placements and audio recordings you created, (c) multimedia materials created on the computer, and (d) photographs of large books.

6. If using a software program, save the file and name it appropriately.

To organize items into categories using Inspiration, simply open the table of contents file (in Outline View) that was created if you used Inspiration in Activity 7.1. Then, create subtopics under each main category and type the titles of the items you wish to include under the appropriate category (see Figure 7.2 for an example). Move the subcategories and items as needed. Remember to save the file with a new version name!

Whether you used the low- or high-tech option, the end result will be a comprehensive list of the contents of each category in the table of contents. We recommend that you create the categories and the contents of each in digital format, as it will be easy to convert the list into a helpful navigational tool at later points in the design phase. One way to accomplish this task is to type the name of each category, a description of the items in the category, and the names of the individual items included in each into a word processor, HTML editor, or other type of software program. Then, make sure you save your file.

## Storyboarding

Once you have developed your table of contents, you are ready to begin creating the storyboard. The storyboard is a visual plan or sketch of your digital teaching portfolio. The process of creating a storyboard will force you to think about how you plan on presenting information about your credentials in the digital teaching portfolio. The storyboard itself demonstrates the layout of the portfolio and the expectation of how viewers will move, or navigate, various parts of the portfolio.

Information presented in digital format can be presented in two different styles—linear and nonlinear. If information is presented in a linear style, the reader will navigate from one Web page or slide to the next in a sequence controlled by the designer. If information is presented in a nonlinear style, the portfolio may be navigated in many different sequences as controlled by the viewer. Figure 7.3 is an ex-

**+ Table of Contents**
- **I.** **+ Classroom Environment**
  - **A.** – Seating chart
  - **B.** – Classroom management plan
- **II.** **+ Assessment Plan**
  - **A.** + Performance-based assessment
    - **1.** – Classification of rocks example
  - **B.** + Student Work Samples
    - **1.** – Reflective statements
  - **C.** – Principal's commentary on assessment plan
- **III.** **+ Professional Development**
  - **A.** – Short-& long-term goals
  - **B.** – Workshops attended this year
- **IV.** **+ Curriculum Development**
  - **A.** – Long-term plans for year
  - **B.** – Recycling unit
- **V.** **+ Theory**
  - **A.** – PowerPoint presentation on learning theories
  - **B.** – Educational philosophy statement

*Source:* This outline was created using Inspiration® by Inspiration®, Inc.

FIGURE 7.2  Using Inspiration to Group Artifacts (Outline View)

ample of a linear design structure. In this example, viewers must move from one page or slide to the next; they cannot move to a particular page out of sequence.

We recommend that you create a portfolio that uses a nonlinear navigation style. This style will enable viewers to determine how they want to navigate information in your portfolio. Viewers will be able to go directly where they need to go in your portfolio to find specific information about you. Of the software programs reviewed in Chapter 11, Kid Pix is the only one that does not support nonlinear navigation.

An additional note: Any software that allows you to present information in a nonlinear navigation style can be adapted so that information can be accessed in a linear style as well. However, the converse is not true. Software that presents information in a linear style cannot be adapted to a nonlinear style.

If you develop your digital teaching portfolio around a nonlinear navigation style, there are several different ways you can structure your information. The most popular are the branching and star structures (see Figure 7.4). The structure selec-

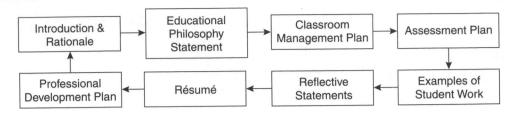

FIGURE 7.3   Linear Design Structure

tion you choose may be based on the amount of information you have and your skills as a designer.

If you followed our instructions for organizing resources by creating categories for a table of contents and deciding on the contents of each category, then storyboarding will be an easy task. Complete Activity 7.3 to create the storyboard of your digital teaching portfolio using paper and pencil. Or, use the same general strategies in the activity to create your storyboard using Inspiration (or other software program).

## Activity 7.3

### CREATING YOUR STORYBOARD USING PAPER AND PENCIL

1. Take a large piece of butcher paper (any piece will work even if one side has already been used) and sit with it in front of you.
2. Take the various card categories (on index cards or sticky notes) and move them around the area until each appears in the place where you would like it to be located in your digital teaching portfolio.
3. Tape each index card or sticky note to the area representing where you would like it to appear. If you want, you can then draw arrows demonstrating how users will navigate this information.
4. To take storyboarding one step further, get enough blank pieces of paper to represent each of the materials you described on your index cards. This paper will represent each page, resource, or "node" of information in your portfolio.
5. On the paper, draw a visual sketch of how the resource (whether artifact or supporting documentation) will appear on this page. In your drawing, be as detailed as possible. Include how information will be aligned and feel free to include drawings of the graphics you would like to include (see Chapter 13 for information on the principles of graphic design). Do not let your current knowledge and skill level influence your sketches. If you cannot accomplish the plans you set out in your sketches, hang onto them for later. You may develop the expertise to achieve your plans sooner than you think! Also, do not let the availability of clip art and other graphics influence whether you include these in your plan for each page or not.

Even if you do not have access to the hardware or software to make your dreams a reality at the moment, you may eventually. Drawing out your plans on paper does not mean that you will execute them all. Page sketches can serve as blueprints of your portfolio's progress for years to come.

It is important to note that both the table of contents and the storyboard are merely planning tools that can and probably will be changed. Think of a curriculum you have designed. Did you always follow the plan? Probably not. However, both you and your students probably benefited from your planning efforts.

*Star Structure*

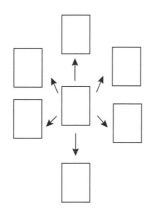

*Branching Structure*

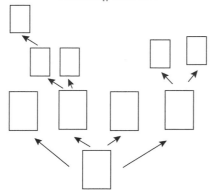

FIGURE 7.4 Nonlinear Design Structures

# Before Producing Your Digital Teaching Portfolio

Once you have developed the table of contents and the storyboard for your digital teaching portfolio, you will be ready to transform this plan into a compilation of digital files provided you have already taken care of several things. At some point (and if not before, then definitely now!), you will have to make a decision about the software or design tool you will use to assemble your portfolio. Chapter 11 has some useful information that you should consider before selecting a design tool. Various factors will serve as the basis for your choice, including your skill level, access to software, the software's capabilities, and the storage medium you will use to share your digital teaching portfolio materials with others.

You will also want to make sure that all of your materials are in a digital format that is compatible with the design tool you are using to develop your digital teaching portfolio. You may need to convert materials into digital format if they were not created using a computer or if they were created in a digital format this is not compatible with the software program you have selected. For example, you may want to include a collage that you or your students have made. To do so, you will need to scan the collage and save it in a digital format (e.g., .jpg,.gif, .bmp). The format will depend on the software program you are using. We recommend you review the user's manual of your chosen software program to learn which file formats it can accept (or review the different file formats we list under popular programs for developing a digital teaching portfolio in Chapter 11). If at all possible, convert materials into digital files gradually as you collect them to reduce your workload and the energy this tedious task requires.

Finally, you will want to make sure that you have determined the resources you will require for your work and have made provisions to access them. The resources you might need may range from a simple computer and software program to more advanced equipment, to people who might help you develop the digital teaching portfolio. The software you choose to create your portfolio will determine your hardware, software, and personnel needs. For example, if you choose to create a Web-based digital teaching portfolio with pictures and video, then you will need to have access to a multimedia computer, software, and digital video equipment.

If you do not own this hardware and software, your school, school district, and/or university with which you are affiliated may be a good place to start looking for what you need. Do not limit your ideas for your digital teaching portfolio to the hardware and software that you already know how to use. Creating your portfolio might be a *great* excuse for developing new technology-related knowledge and even give you the opportunity to purchase new hardware and software. Use Figure 7.5 to determine some of the resources you might need to develop your digital teaching portfolio.

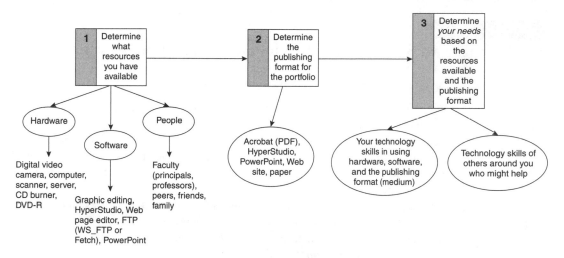

FIGURE 7.5 Resources Needed for Creating Your Digital Teaching Portfolio

# Producing Your Digital Teaching Portfolio

Regardless of the design tool you are using, there will come a point in the production process when each item in your portfolio will become either one part of a larger digital file making up your portfolio (i.e., if you are using HyperStudio, PowerPoint, or Kid Pix) or one file in a collection of files that make up your portfolio (i.e., if you are using Adobe Acrobat, Netscape Composer, or another HTML editing program).

Several strategies exist for creating digital files, but not all will save you time and promote consistency in the graphic design of every page or slide of your portfolio. Because each software program works differently, we present a strategy that will work with most programs used to create a digital teaching portfolio: the creation of a template file. Creating a template file consists of several steps:

1. The creation of a "master" or "template" file that has settings for all the graphic elements of a page or slide, which becomes the preset or "model" page or slide for the portfolio
2. The saving of this file with the name "master" or "template"
3. The testing of the template file to determine whether all of its features work
4. The creation of each new file from the master template file
5. The saving of each new file with a new name

Complete Activity 7.4 to create a template using the software program you have chosen for creating your digital teaching portfolio.

## Activity 7.4

### CREATING A TEMPLATE FOR YOUR DIGITAL TEACHING PORTFOLIO

Creating a template file is fairly simple. Just follow these steps:

1. Open the program you plan to use for creating your digital teaching portfolio (e.g., PowerPoint or Composer).
2. Decide on the standard graphic elements you will include on every page of your portfolio. Standard graphic elements you might include are the background color, background design, a logo, a menu, a table of contents, the date of production, page title, etc.
3. Create a page/slide that has all of these elements and save it twice. Save it once with the name "template" and once with the name "template_back_up." This may seem silly, but you would be amazed to know how many times we have accidentally saved over our original template file!
4. Test or double check the template file to make sure it works properly so as to avoid replicating mistakes contained in the template file by:
   - Ensuring that all of the links work
   - Making sure all graphics and text are exactly where you want them
   - Conducting a spell check
   - Proofreading for any grammatical errors
   - Testing the template using different platforms (e.g., Mac, PC), versions of operating systems (e.g., Mac OS 8.2, Windows XP), and browsers (e.g., Internet Explorer, Netscape Composer)
5. Open the template file and make any modifications that customize the file. This will involve copying and pasting or merging the contents of an artifact in digital format with the template file.
6. Finally save the file with a *new name* so that the template file will remain unchanged. Refer to Chapter 10 for suggestions for naming files.

Here are some words of caution for you. It is essential that you refine and check your template file before using it as the basis for creating any other pages or slides. If you create a template file with mistakes, you will replicate the mistake in every file you create from the template. Fixing the same mistake on every file in your digital teaching portfolio (e.g., a misspelled word in your table of contents) is tedious and time-consuming, So take the time to make sure the template file is flawless!

## PowerPoint

If you are using Microsoft PowerPoint to create your digital teaching portfolio, you will most likely create individual "slides" for each of the categories in the table of contents. In cases where there are too many items for one slide presentation, you may have to create several PowerPoint slide presentations that are linked together. If you plan to present your materials in linear style, you can use the program's default settings. However, if you wish to present your materials in a nonlinear style, you will need to use the program's "hyperlink" feature (available in the PowerPoint '97 or higher versions for PC and version 7 or higher for Mac). Using the hyperlink feature, it is possible to create a table of contents that is linked to different slides in the digital teaching portfolio.

One of PowerPoint's features is the ability to create a "master" slide. We suggest that you use this feature to create a template if you are using PowerPoint. Also, we recommend that you save your portfolio in such a way so that people with different versions of PowerPoint will be able to open your portfolio. To do this, select "Save As," type in the title of the file, and select the option that allows you to save the file in as many formats as possible. For example, if you are using PowerPoint 2000, we suggest that you save the file as a "PowerPoint 2000 Presentation."

## HTML (Netscape Composer)

If you are creating your digital teaching portfolio in HTML format, then you will need to turn each category or each file containing the resource represented by that category into its own HTML file. These files will then need to be linked together from the table of contents and from the individual pages if you choose.

If your files are already in a digital format compatible with the word processing program Microsoft Word, then use the file conversion feature that enables you to easily save the files in HTML format. Once you have the files in HTML format, you will be able to close them and open them in Netscape Composer or any another HTML editing program to link them to one another and to add features such as graphics and colored backgrounds.

## SUMMARY

In this chapter, we described the third stage of the digital teaching portfolio development process, the design stage. In this stage, the portfolio developer organizes materials by developing a table of contents and storyboard. Various methods exist to facilitate this process. Index cards, sticky notes, or computer software programs can be used to help teachers visualize the organization and flow of materials in the portfolio. Once these steps are completed, various software programs are used to produce the portfolio. The procedures for producing the various resources for inclusion in the portfolio vary depending on the software program that is used. Tips were presented for creating a digital teaching portfolio with PowerPoint and Netscape Composer. Creation of a template or "master document" can facilitate the production of a digital teaching portfolio.

## CHECK YOUR UNDERSTANDING

1. What are the steps of the design stage of the digital teaching portfolio development process?
2. What is the purpose of storyboarding?
3. Describe one strategy for creating a storyboard for your digital teaching portfolio.
4. What is the difference between linear and nonlinear navigation style? What are the advantages and disadvantages of each navigation style?
5. Why is it useful to create a digital teaching portfolio using a template?

# Evaluating Your Digital Teaching Portfolio

## eight

In recent years, the word "evaluation" has developed a bad connotation. However, evaluation is not a four-letter word. Evaluating your digital teaching portfolio is an important part of the portfolio creation process. In this chapter, we will discuss how careful evaluation can help you create a more professional portfolio by providing you with useful information.

## Portfolios and Evaluation

Evaluation is a critical part of the development of any instructional material. Whether you have considered it or not, your digital teaching portfolio *is* an instructional material. It may even be one of the most important instructional materials you will ever create! Your digital teaching portfolio serves to teach others about your professional competence. Because you are a teacher, the ease, speed, and depth with which your portfolio teaches others about your capabilities is as important an indication of your competence as the actual artifacts it contains.

Evaluation may be used for several purposes when performed in association with your digital teaching portfolio. You may evaluate your own portfolio to determine how well it functions as an instructional tool (i.e., how well it teaches others about you as a teacher). Formative and summative evaluation will help you do this (we discuss these in the sections that follow). Your portfolio can also allow others, such as principals and teacher education professors, to evaluate your ability as an educator and discern the level of your professional competence. This evaluation will be based on the evidence communicated in the artifacts included in your portfolio and your reflection on these artifacts. Evaluation also can enable others to examine the work you put into the process of creating a portfolio, providing yet another picture of you. Evaluation of your portfolio will involve many people and guidelines. In this chapter, we present some evaluation methods that we have found to be useful during the creation of digital teaching portfolios. Keep in mind, however, that a thorough discussion of the evaluation of teaching portfolios is beyond the scope of this book.

# Evaluating Your Digital Teaching Portfolio

There are two kinds of evaluation: formative and summative. Both methods of evaluation play important roles in the digital teaching portfolio development process. Help from others is essential for both types of evaluation to be useful to you because designers have difficulty being constructively critical of their own work.

Formative evaluation is evaluation that occurs during the development of instructional materials. The goal of formative evaluation is to determine whether the materials fulfill the intended purpose. The purpose or objectives of the materials are central to this type of evaluation. To understand formative evaluation, imagine a chef tasting a soup while she is cooking it. Because the soup is still in its formative stage, the chef can change the recipe as needed to improve the soup. If the chef's goal is to produce a tasty soup, then all evaluation revolves around investigating this characteristic—not texture or color of the soup.

Summative evaluation is performed after development of an instructional material is complete. The focus of this evaluation is to determine the quality of the instructional materials. Quality is usually measured by how well something compares with a certain set of standards. To understand summative evaluation, imagine a crowd at a dinner party tasting and deciding how well they like the soup the chef has made. At this point, it is too late for the chef to improve the soup. It is left up to the crowd to judge its quality. They each have ideas about what quality means. Each will decide how well the soup measures up to their idea of what soup should taste like, look like, and smell like. Then, sometimes the crowd will make a judgement about how good the chef is based on her soup.

# Conducting Formative Evaluation on Your Digital Teaching Portfolio

When you ask friends, colleagues, students, or other people you know for input on the your digital teaching portfolio while it is in one of the development stages, you are conducting an informal, formative evaluation. If you take time to carefully formulate the questions you ask these helpful individuals, you will raise the level of your evaluation to a more formal level. Doing this will yield better information for your effort.

Figure 8.1 provides some of the areas about which you will want to elicit information from your reviewers. The areas relate to the stages of portfolio development.

You also will want to investigate the digital teaching portfolio for its ability to present ideas well through its graphic design, its technical requirements (e.g., Is it viewable on various machines? Does it cause crashes? Can it be viewed easily?), Is

**FIGURE 8.1**  Questions for Conducting a Formative Evaluation

**Step 1: Planning—Frame and Focus**

The focus and framework should be apparent to the viewer through their interactions with the digital teaching portfolio materials—no guesswork should be involved. Does the portfolio have a focus and framework? Does it cater to a specific audience? Can you guess the characteristics of the audience by looking at the portfolio? Does the portfolio cater to the attributes of this group? What could be improved to make it better suited to the audience?

**Step 2: Considering Digital Teaching Portfolio Materials—Collecting, Selecting, and Reflecting**

Do the materials match the intended focus and framework? Are they presented in a way that appeals to the viewer? Do the reflections make sense? Are they all accounted for or are enough included for the moment? What more could be added?

**Step 3: Designing—Organizing and Producing**

Is like information grouped together? Is the portfolio easy to understand and navigate? What is behind certain category titles? Is it organized? Does the linear/non-linear navigation system work? Does the software program used for presentation of materials do its job? Does it work for viewers with various hardware and software configurations? Does it work the same way on every machine/operating system/version of the software?

**Step 4: Publishing**

Does the published medium work whether on CD, Web, etc.? Will it work for members of the intended audience? How could it be made more useable?

it culturally sensitive (e.g., Does it portray different cultures or gender appropriately?), and its ability to communicate the personality of the teacher.

To help you conduct the formative evaluation of your digital teaching portfolio, we encourage you to find at least one critical friend. A critical friend is someone you trust who will provide you with *constructive criticism* of your portfolio, listen to your needs and questions, and direct you to where you can find more help. In our experience, critical friends have been our peers, principals, professors, significant others, and even our very own parents. Some portfolio developers involve friends from the beginning, whereas others involve their critical friends only at the very end. The amount of involvement that a critical friend has is up to the developer and time constraints. More on how to do a formative evaluation is presented in Activity 8.1.

## Activity 8.1

### FORMATIVE EVALUATION OF YOUR DIGITAL TEACHING PORTFOLIO

Ask your critical friend(s) to review your digital teaching portfolio to determine if:

1. The portfolio has a focus and framework.
2. All of the artifacts in the portfolio seem to be tied to standards, a theme, or a question.
3. The portfolio is easy to navigate and understand.
4. The portfolio encourages the reader to learn more about you and your teaching.
5. The portfolio needs additional revision (for grammatical, spelling, and syntax errors).
6. The portfolio is cohesive and various components seem connected.

Discuss these issues with your critical friend to learn where your digital teaching portfolio's strengths and weaknesses are and how you might improve the portfolio as a whole. You may want your critical friend to use the sample formative evaluation (see Figure 8.2 in this text) or ask him to share his comments.

FIGURE 8.2   Sample Formative Evaluation

| | |
|---|---|
| One to Flow On | What is most effective about this digital teaching portfolio? |
| One to Grow On | What suggestion(s) do you have to improve the digital teaching portfolio? |
| One to Think About | What questions do you still have? |
| One to Take Home | What is one thing you learned as a result of reviewing this digital teaching portfolio? |

# Conducting the Summative Evaluation of Your Digital Teaching Portfolio

Although many people will examine a teacher's digital teaching portfolio to make judgements about how competent her teaching is, the evaluation of a portfolio really only tells you about the portfolio itself. Even though it is possible to make generalizations about someone's teaching competence based on his performance as it is demonstrated in a portfolio, it is impossible to really know about a person's teaching competence without actually witnessing and experiencing the teacher in the classroom.

In considering how a portfolio should be evaluated in a summative way, a rubric may be useful. A rubric can measure how well someone performed the steps of the digital teaching portfolio development process and how thorough his communication of various documents is. The rubric might measure:

- Growth (from start to finish of the portfolio)
- Accomplishment of specific standards as evidenced in artifacts and reflections
- Technology skills incorporated into the design of the portfolio (or those not incorporated)
- The process in retrospect to see what the teacher gained from it
- The product as it relates to the steps of the digital teaching portfolio development process

For more on the summative evaluation process, see Activity 8.2.

## Activity 8.2

### SUMMATIVE EVALUATION OF YOUR DIGITAL TEACHING PORTFOLIO

For the summative evaluation, we suggest you use a rubric (a rubric also can be used for the formative evaluation). A rubric is a set of scoring guidelines based on established criteria for evaluating one's work. Use the summative evaluation rubric (see Figure 8.3) and the summative evaluation form (see Figure 8.4) we have developed to evaluate your portfolio. Ask a critical friend to use the rubric for scoring your portfolio and the form for writing comments and suggestions.

FIGURE 8.3   Sample Summative Evaluation Rubric

|  | Outstanding | Very Good | Good | Needs Work |
|---|---|---|---|---|
| **Organization** | ■ Very well organized and presented | ■ Well organized and presented | ■ Organized and orderly | ■ Poorly organized and presented |
| **Portfolio framework** | ■ Very clearly aligned with and demonstrates competence in the portfolio's stated focus and frame | ■ Clearly aligned with and demonstrates competence in the portfolio's stated focus and frame | ■ Aligned with and demonstrates competence in the portfolio's stated focus and frame | ■ Not clearly aligned with and does not demonstrate competence in the portfolio's stated focus and frame |
| **Design** | ■ Keen attention to design issues (alignment, contrast, proximity, repetition)<br>■ Very easy to understand<br>■ Very easy to navigate<br>■ Looks very professional<br>■ All links work<br>■ Designed for people with disabilities | ■ Attention to design issues (alignment, contrast, proximity, repetition)<br>■ Easy to understand<br>■ Easy to navigate<br>■ Looks professional<br>■ Most links work<br>■ Designed for people with disabilities | ■ Some attention to design issues (alignment, contrast, proximity, repetition)<br>■ Understandable<br>■ Navigable<br>■ Somewhat professional<br>■ Few links work<br>■ Not designed for people with disabilities | ■ No attention to design issues (alignment, contrast, proximity, repetition)<br>■ Difficult to understand<br>■ Difficult to navigate<br>■ Looks unprofessional<br>■ Several links work<br>■ Not designed for people with disabilities |
| **Mechanics (spelling, grammar, syntax)** | ■ No spelling, grammar, or syntax errors | ■ Few spelling, grammar, and syntax errors | ■ Some spelling, grammar, and syntax errors | ■ Many spelling, grammar, and syntax errors<br>■ Not carefully selected items |
| **Contents** | ■ Very carefully selected items<br>■ Very appropriate to focus and frame<br>■ Very comprehensive | ■ Carefully selected items<br>■ Appropriate to focus and frame<br>■ Comprehensive | ■ Somewhat carefully selected items<br>■ Somewhat appropriate to focus and frame<br>■ Somewhat comprehensive | ■ Inappropriate to focus and frame<br>■ Not comprehensive |

FIGURE 8.4  Sample Summative Evaluation Form

**How do you rate this digital teaching portfolio? (check one)**

❏ Outstanding
❏ Very Good
❏ Good
❏ Needs Work

**Why did you rate the digital teaching portfolio in this manner?**

**Please write additional comments or suggestions below.**

# Revising Your Digital Teaching Portfolio

Revision is an ongoing part of the digital teaching portfolio development process. In fact, because we like to consider digital teaching portfolios as works-in-progress (Aren't teachers always developing and growing?), we believe digital teaching portfolios can always use a little tinkering and improvement. After you have asked your critical friend(s) to review your portfolio, reflect upon their comments and suggestions and make any necessary changes.

## SUMMARY

In this chapter, we presented information on the important role evaluation plays in developing a digital teaching portfolio. Formative evaluation is part of an ongoing process intended to improve the quality of your portfolio during its development. Friends, colleagues, and even students might be helpful in this evaluation. As information is elicited from those helping with formative evaluation, it can be used to revise your portfolio. Because of formative evaluation, the portfolio process is recursive that is, it cycles through different stages in continual improvement. The purpose of summative evaluation is to determine the quality of the portfolio product. Summative evaluation should provide information about how effective your portfolio communicates the focus and framework of the portfolio and how well it communicates your goals as a whole. One effective way to evaluate a portfolio is through the use of a rubric.

## CHECK YOUR UNDERSTANDING

1. What is the difference between formative evaluation and summative evaluation? Use an analogy to illustrate.

2. What are some ways you can evaluate your digital teaching portfolio?

## nine

# Publishing Your Digital Teaching Portfolio

Although you will benefit from the process of simply creating your digital tcachng portfolio and evaluating it, you will experience even greater benefits if you share the portfolio you have created with others. Publishing your portfolio will enable you to do this. In this chapter, we will explain the various options that exist for publishing and sharing your work with others.

## Options for Publishing Your Digital Teaching Portfolio

You have several options for publishing your digital teaching portfolio and more are being created every day as technological applications supporting digital portfolio production evolve. Each option makes your portfolio available to those with whom you would like to share it, but does so in different ways. These are your basic options:

■ You can use File Transfer Protocol (FTP) to copy the digital teaching portfolio to a server so that it is accessible on the World Wide Web. This option makes your portfolio accessible to anyone who has an Internet service provider (ISP) and a Web browser.

■ You can save the portfolio on a storage device such as a CD, DVD, or Zip disk. Floppy disks could be used, but generally they do not have the storage space to contain small portfolios. This option makes your portfolio accessible to whomever you give a copy provided they meet two requirements. First, depending on the media you use, they must have a computer that has a CD-R/CD-RW, DVD-R/DVD-RW, or Zip drive. Second, they must have appropriate software installed on their computer. They need either the same software program you used to create your portfolio or software "helper" application that allows them to view the files you created. This software is often called a plug-in or "reader." Such software is generally provided for free on the Internet or it can be packaged along with the portfolio and installed.

■ You can print a hard copy of your portfolio and provide hard copies to anyone you like.

Each of these options is described further in the following sections.

# Publishing Your Digital Teaching Portfolio on the World Wide Web Using FTP

Publishing a portfolio on the World Wide Web is getting easier and easier. However, there are certain things you need to know to do the job. You will need to have designated server space to FTP or upload your digital teaching portfolio to the server. Depending on where you upload your portfolio, you also may need to use one of several software programs to transfer the files (e.g., Fetch, http://www.fetchsoftworks.com, for the Mac or WS_FTP, http://www.ftphelp.com, for the PC). Several HTML or Web editing programs allow you to FTP your files directly to a server without the use of a separate FTP program (such as Dreamweaver).

If you are a teacher candidate or inservice teacher, you probably have (or can request) space allocated on a server at your school or with your school district. Use of this space likely has certain rules and guidelines associated with it. If not, you might want to register for free server space or use an ISP. If you have control of your own server space, you can upload and download whenever you need or want. This allows you to modify the portfolio any way you like at any time.

No matter how you FTP your files, (using WS_FTP, Fetch, or an HTML editing program), there is certain information you will need to know to upload and download files to a server. You will need the following information to successfully FTP your portfolio:

■ Server address (e.g., www.webserveraddress.com)
■ Log in (identification)

- Password
    Some Web sites that offer free or inexpensive server space are:
- AngelCities: http://www.angelcities.com
- Angelfire: http://www.angelfire.com
- Yahoo!GeoCities: http://geocities.yahoo.com
- Homestead: http://www.homestead.com
- Netscape: http://home.netscape.com/websites/index.html

We encourage you to explore the options available on each of these sites to determine which might best fit your needs. For reviews of free Web hosts, read http://www.ftpplanet.com/cgi/_listreview/listreview.pl?list_path=Web_free_hosting. At this site you can read customer reviews of the hosting sites and learn how they are rated.

If you have (and pay for) an ISP such as America Online, AT&T Worldnet, Earthlink, Erols, Mindspring, or Prodigy, you can upload your digital teaching portfolio to server space. Each of these service providers offers Web server space to its subscribers. Once you have uploaded your digital teaching portfolio and all the associated files, you should check each page to ensure that all of the links and graphics are loading well.

The key to transferring your files to a server is making sure that you upload all of the files to the correct directories and subdirectories (sometimes called folders and subfolders). Review the section on testing your portfolio for more on checking your portfolio.

# Publishing Your Digital Teaching Portfolio on a CD or DVD

To publish your digital teaching portfolio onto a CD or DVD, you will need the appropriate hardware, such as a CD-R (CD-Record) or DVD-RW (DVD-Rewritable) drive (see Chapter 12 for more on hardware), and software (should come with the drive) to save your files onto CD or DVD.

Whichever drive and software program you use, we highly recommend you create a hybrid CD. A hybrid CD is one that can be read on both Mac and PC. The CD-R or CD-RW drive burns (or etches) data onto the CD using a laser.

Some CD and DVD record and rewrite drives have "packet writing" software that allows you to save your files in the same way that you would on a floppy disk. On the other hand, many drives do not support packet writing. With drives that do not support packet writing, once you save files to a CD, you can not save on the same CD again. Check the manuals (drive and software) to see how to save files onto a CD or DVD and to learn whether the drive you have supports packet writing.

# Publishing Your Digital Teaching Portfolio on a Zip or Floppy Disk

Publishing your digital teaching portfolio to a Zip or floppy disk is very easy. Just insert a Zip or floppy disk into the appropriate drive and drag a copy of your entire portfolio onto the disk. Once you save it, you can give a copy of your digital teaching portfolio to anyone who has the equipment and software to view your portfolio (see Chapters 11 and 12 for information on software and hardware).

An important note: Zip disks are platformcentric. This means that a Mac formatted Zip disk cannot be read on a PC. Fortunately, newer versions of the Macintosh operating system (7.5 and newer) can read PC-formatted Zip disks. To avoid problems of file incompatibility, use PC-formatted Zip disks whether working on a PC or a Mac. Also, keep in mind the type of Zip drive you own and the disks it uses. A 250 megabyte (MB) Zip disk will not run in a 100 MB Zip drive; however, the opposite will (a 100 MB Zip in a 250 MB drive). Therefore, it is important to use Zip disks keeping in mind the type of computer viewers will be viewing your portfolio on.

# Publishing Your Digital Teaching Portfolio on Paper

The last option we will discuss is publishing your digital teaching portfolio on paper. Although this approach does not offer many of the advantages that producing a portfolio in digital format offers, it is a worthwhile option for several reasons.

First, publishing your portfolio on paper makes it accessible to everyone regardless of whether they have access to a computer or not. Second, it is a method of publishing available to teachers who do not have access to hardware equipment that stores large files. Third, paper publishing is easy and feasible for teachers who are only beginning to develop their technical skills. Fourth, this method still enables designers to utilize some of the advantages of using a computer to produce a neat, visually appealing piece of work. Paper publishing of digital teaching portfolios allows easy reproduction of materials, and it promotes creativity while supporting the use of many different software tools (image editing programs, page layout programs, etc.). Finally, publishing a digital teaching portfolio on paper provides teachers an opportunity to begin "getting their feet wet" with technological tools.

To publish your digitial teaching portfolio, you would simply print out copies of each page in your portfolio. Then you would compile them in a binder or other storage container.

Depending on the program you used to create your portfolio, you may have different options for printing your portfolio. For example, to print a portfolio created in PowerPoint, you have several options. The options are to print:

- Individual slides (prints one slide per page)
- Handouts (two, three, or six slides per page)
- Notes Pages (prints the individual slide and the notes you wrote under each one)
- Outline View (prints the outline only)

However, if you wish to print a portfolio that was created using a Web editor, then you should open each file of your portfolio in a Web browser and print it. Or, simply open the main file (probably the home.html file) and print each page.

# Testing Your Portfolio

After you have saved a copy of your entire digital teaching portfolio (including any supporting files), examine your entire portfolio. If you created a portfolio that can be viewed on the Web, then test every single image link and page to ensure that all graphics appear the way you want and that all links are all working correctly. We recommend that you review your portfolio using different platforms (i.e., Mac, PC), operating systems (i.e., Mac OS 8.1, Windows XP), versions of software (i.e., PowerPoint 97, PowerPoint 2000), and the two common Internet browsers (i.e., Internet Explorer, Netscape Navigator) if you have created a Web-based digital teaching portfolio. You may notice minor (or major) differences in the appearance of your portfolio when using different hardware and software configurations. We urge you to test your digital teaching portfolio to ensure that it works and looks exactly the way you want it to look.

Why go through the trouble to test your site on different platforms, operating systems, browsers, and software versions? Well, because it is difficult to say exactly what platform, operating system, browser, and software version the people with whom you share your portfolio will use to view it. That is exactly why we recommend creating Web-based digital teaching portfolios—they are accessible to practically anyone with a Web browser and an Internet connection!

## SUMMARY

In this chapter, we discuss various approaches you might choose from when publishing your digital teaching portfolio. Each option requires different equipment, knowledge, and skills, but each influences the way members of your audience will experience your portfolio. Options for publishing include saving it to a Zip disk, CD, or DVD, uploading it to server space on the World Wide Web, or printing it on paper. Intstructions describing how to carry out each of these options are provided.

## CHECK YOUR UNDERSTANDING

1. What are the different methods you can use for publishing your digital teaching portfolio?
2. What free server space might educators use to store their portfolios?
3. What hardware and software are required to publish a portfolio to CD or DVD?
4. Why is it important to test your site?

# Thinking about Putting "Digital" into Your Teaching Portfolio

In the forthcoming chapters, we provide guidelines for teachers to consider before designing a digital teaching portfolio. Chapter 10 outlines the "Digital Teaching Portfolio Commandments." These are some general guidelines for making the digital teaching portfolio development process run more smoothly. The commandments address organizational strategies, security concerns, and issues of authorship and privacy that should be considered before, during, and after you create the portfolio. Chapter 11 describes some popular software programs for designing digital teaching portfolios, as well as some of the pros and cons of each of these applications. Chapter 12 defines many of the hardware options available and offers our recommendations for selecting hardware to create a digital teaching portfolio. Although the hardware descriptions are not exhaustive, there should be enough information to help teachers make sound decisions about the equipment that they choose to create their portfolios. Finally, Chapter 13 describes the basic elements of graphic design. Understanding the elements of graphic design will help teachers to make informed decisions about the visual appearance of their digital teaching portfolios.

# Things to Consider Before and After Getting Started

Most teachers, either by necessity or personal preference, are pack rats. It is not unusual for their desk drawers, closets, basements, and car trunks to be full to overflowing with what will make excellent artifacts when included in a digital teaching portfolio. Of course, some people might call the egg cartons, book collections, lesson plans, and student projects a four-letter word starting with "J"—but we know better! These things might be considered treasures with sentimental value, but they are also evidence of hard work and professionalism.

Before accumulating and organizing these artifacts, it is wise to do some homework and preplanning. We all know too well that even the best plans do not always turn out as intended. This chapter will present some things to do and issues to consider before you even begin assembling your digital teaching portfolio that will make the process easier and save you a lot of time and headaches. We are calling these tips the

"Digital Teaching Portfolio Commandments." These are good rules to live by for organizing and saving any work that you do.

# The Digital Teaching Portfolio Commandments

## 1. When in Doubt, DON'T Throw It Out

You never know what you might want to include in your digital teaching portfolio. Even that horrible lesson plan that bombed might be something it would be wise to consider. It might demonstrate how much you learned from the experience. Or, it could represent a turning point in your development as a teacher. Just like diamonds, ordinary items that withstand the test of time might turn out to be useful and beautiful!

## 2. Do It Digital

Although there will always be a place for original or hard copy documents, archiving documents in digital format is becoming more and more common. Information stored in digital format takes up less physical space, does not degrade in quality (although the storage format in which it is saved may deteriorate over time and under certain environmental conditions), and has the advantage of being easier to share with numerous people. Thus, it makes sense to save your work in a digital format.

Whenever possible, save work in a digital format that transfers easily to the Web. Regardless of the format you intend to use when displaying your digital teaching portfolio, saving files to Web-compatible formats will increase the likelihood that your files will be able to be read for years to come using simple Web browsing software such as Netscape Navigator and Internet Explorer. Although most software programs do change and evolve as new technology develops, formats supported by the World Wide Web have proliferated to the extent that they have become the accepted "standard" for digital archiving. File formats that can be read or easily converted to files that can be used on the Web are listed in Table 10.1.

More and more software programs are including features that enable you to save files automatically to html format (e.g., HyperStudio and those in the Microsoft Office Suite). Saving in HTML format now will minimize the work required later. The following URL provides links to sites that explain nearly every file format imaginable: http://whatis.techtarget.com/fileFormatA/0,289933,sid9,00.html.

Saving your files in digital format will likely reduce the amount of work you will be required to do when you compile and assemble your portfolio. Minimizing the tiresome work of saving and converting files will allow you to spend more time reflecting on your work and presenting it in interesting, creative ways.

Take advantage of capturing files in digital format. You can have photos devel-

TABLE 10.1

## Recommended File Formats for Saving Artifacts

| Artifact Examples | Recommended File Format |
|---|---|
| Awards<br>Case studies<br>Educational philosophy<br>  statement<br>Evaluations<br>Lesson plans<br>Research papers<br>Résumé<br>Student work | ■ rtf (rich text format): Can be read by most word processing programs<br>■ pdf (Portable Document Format): Can be read on the WWW, requires the use of Adobe Acrobat or Acrobat Reader (free)<br>■ HTML (Hypertext Markup Language): Can be read on the WWW using a Web browser |
| Sound | ■ aif (Audio Interchange File): One of two popular sound file formats on Apple Macintosh<br>■ aiff (Audio Interchange File Format): One of two popular sound file formats on Apple Macintosh<br>■ midi (Musical Instrument Digital Interface): Used to create music files, can be played or downloaded from the WWW with most browsers and a player<br>■ mp3 (MPEG-1 Audio Layer-3): This format compresses files into much smaller ones, files are usually downloaded (not streamed), can be played or downloaded from the WWW with most browsers and a player<br>■ ra (Real Audio): Allows you to play sound instantaneously rather having to wait for the sound file to download completely (as in a .wav file), can be heard on the WWW with most browsers and Real Audio player<br>■ wav (Waveform Sound for Microsoft Windows): Standard PC audio format that also can be used with Mac, can be downloaded from the WWW |
| Video | ■ avi (Microsoft Audio Video Interleaved file): For Windows movie, can be heard on the WWW with most browsers and a player<br>■ mpeg or mpg (Moving Picture Experts Group): This format compresses both audio and video files, can be viewed/heard on the WWW using an mpeg player<br>■ mov (QuickTime for Microsoft Windows): See qt below<br>■ ram (Real Audio Metafile): See ra above<br>■ rm (Real Audio video file): See ra above<br>■ rv (Real Video): see ra above<br>■ qt (QuickTime): Allows for development, storage, and playback of movies, developed by Apple, can be viewed on the WWW using a QuickTime player |
| Graphics<br>Photographs | ■ jpg or jpeg (Joint Photographic Experts Group): Supports 24-bit color (16 million colors). It is a good choice for photos. Can be viewed on the WWW using a Web browser or using a software program for viewing such files.<br>■ gif (Graphic Interchange Format): Supports 8-bit (256) color. It is a good choice for line art, maps, graphics, and drawings. Can be viewed on the WWW using a Web browser or a software program for viewing such files.<br>■ bmp (Windows Bitmap file): Supports 24-bit color and is supported by most Windows programs<br>■ png (Portable Network Graphics): Supports 24-bit color. Can be viewed on the WWW using a Web browser or using a software program for viewing such files. |

oped normally, but you also can have them saved onto a CD, online, or to a floppy disk in jpg format. This can save time; you will not have to scan that great picture if you have already saved it in digital (jpg) format.

### 3. Be Organized, Not Frustrated

If you cannot find a file, it is as good as gone. Developing a good system for keeping track of your digital files is just as important if not more important than developing a system for tracking hard-copy files. We suggest organizing your digital files just as you would organize regular files in your classroom file cabinet.

Using the file management system that comes with your computer (Windows Explorer on the PC and Finder on the Mac), create folders that pertain to the contents you intend to store within them. Name your file folders with short, intentional names that will remind you of their contents. Do not use spaces in the names of your file folders or files. (This will facilitate the transfer of your files from your local computer to CD or a Web server when the time comes). Substitute an underscore ( _ ) for spaces if you must. For instance, you could save a unit you have created on butterflies that includes lesson plans and handouts created with a word processing program, digital photos, and so on in a folder entitled "butterfly_unit."

Also, keep track of file versions if you change and modify files frequently. We like to use the version numbering system used with software programs. For example, for your educational philosophy statement, you could have several versions, such as: edphil1_0.html, edphil2_1.html, edphil3_0.html. The first number changes each time major changes occur in the document. The second number changes only when there are minor changes to a document. Displaying various versions of important files in your portfolio, such as your philosophy of education, can be an excellent way to display your growth and change as a professional. It also can be a lot of fun to look back and reflect on what you believed and how you expressed your beliefs at different stages of your career.

### 4. Log It or Lose It

Keep track of all of your work (e.g., digital materials, videos, photos, paper, etc.) by maintaining a log sheet, or even better, a database using a software program such as FileMaker Pro (http://www.filemaker.com) or Microsoft Access (http://www.microsoft.com). Even the most organized teachers forget where a particular file is or its most recent version. Organizing your work by creating a good filing system (see Commandment #3) is very useful, but it is even more helpful to be able to find or search on a computer using a database exactly where that recycling unit is (Hmm, did you file it in the 1999 Science folder or the 2000 one?). Table 10.2 illustrates how you might organize a log sheet of your work. The same information also could have been entered and saved in a database program.

TABLE 10.2

**Sample Log Sheet of Artifacts**

| File Name | Date | Artifact | Description | Location |
|-----------|------|----------|-------------|----------|
| me.jpg | 2-10-02 | Collage about me | Collage I created for my reading methods class | Portfolio box, Spring 2002 manila folder, in Mom's garage (home!). Scanned image in Spring 2002 folder in computer (backup on 2002 Zip disk and on server) |
| recycling.html | 9-01-02 | Unit lesson plan on re-cycling | This is my great unit on recycling! | Fall 2001 folder in com-puter (backup on 2002 Zip disk and on server) |
| scifair.html | 10-15-02 | Science fair project ex-ample | Science fair experiment on different fertilizers for growing beans | Backboard in Mom's garage (at home!) Paper in Fall 2002 folder in computer (backup on 2002 Zip disk) |
| res11_01.html | 11-20-03 | Résumé | Résumé for spring break internship | Jobs folder in computer (backup on 2003 Zip disk) |

## 5. If It Is Nice, Save It Thrice

Always keep a few extra copies of your work. You can do this by saving an identi-cal copy—a process called "backing up" your work—onto tapes, Zip disks, floppy disks, CDs, or Web servers. Determining which back-up system works best or is most reliable for you can be difficult. The system that is best for you will rely on how much work you need to save, how much money you have to spend on storage devices, and your level of technical skill. Table 10.3 lists some of the options you have for saving your work. Figure 10.1 lists some file saving strategies.

## 6. Be Careful, Not Sorry! Pay Heed to Legal and Security Concerns.

One of the best things about your digital teaching portfolio is that it allows you to share important information about yourself with the public. One of the worst things about your portfolio is that it makes lots of important information about you ac-cessible to anyone with a computer, a Web browser, and an Internet connection. This being the case, it is important to reflect on how much information and what kind of information you want to share before you share it.

TABLE 10.3

**Options for Saving Your Work**

| Type | Holds | Recommendation | Other |
|------|-------|----------------|-------|
| Web Server | 5–100 MB (depends on how much space you allotted on a server) | Highly recommended | http://www.filesanywhere.com/ http://www.surnameweb.org/freedrive.htm (Here is a list of a few places to back up your portfolio) You may be able to get free server space at your school (university or K–12 school). Just ask the technology person if space is available and how you can upload files to it. |
| Zip disk | 100+ MB | Recommended | Requires a Zip drive, available on many computers or it can be added on by purchasing it separately, long-term reliability is unknown |
| CD | 650 MB | Recommended | Requires special equipment to save |
| DVD | 4.7–17 GB | Recommended | Requires special equipment to save |
| Floppy disk | 1.44 MB | Not recommended | Inexpensive, but not very reliable, may not have enough memory for the entire portfolio |
| Tape | 20–40 GB | Not recommended | Requires special equipment |

In a class we taught on designing digital teaching portfolios, one of our students found out this lesson the hard way. When she e-mailed the URL of her portfolio to her mother, she received a very different reaction than she expected! Rather than being delighted by her daughter's display of professional competence and technical skills, the mother was very upset. She called her daughter immediately to ask her to remove her social security number, phone number, and address from the Web site that displayed her digital teaching portfolio. During the next class, an interesting conversation ensued about what personal information should or should not be included in a digital teaching portfolio.

In addition to determining how much and what kind of information you want to share, you also can determine in what medium you will share it. Decisions you make about the display medium will limit the audience able to access information about you. Although posting your digital teaching portfolio on the Web can make it available to the general public, it is possible to password protect all or part of your site. Additionally, you can create your digital teaching portfolio in a Web-compatible format and save it to CD. This enables your portfolio to be read by anyone with a Web browser, but only those with a copy of your CD will be able to gain access to your materials.

FIGURE 10.1 File Saving Strategies

- Placing the file in a relevant folder or storing it on the desktop until you are able to place it into a relevant folder.
- Saving the file to the correct storage device (hard drive, Zip drive, floppy drive) from the time you initially create and save the file. Then, all subsequent times you save the file, it will make new copies of the file in the place you originally selected. This will minimize the number of duplicate files you have on your system.
- Giving your files short and descriptive names.
- Being organized and consistent with your file naming strategies.
- Giving your file an "extension" suffix such as .jpg, .psd, .doc, .html. This way you will know what type of file it is and what kind of software will open it.
- Getting classroom photos developed in both hard copy and digital format.

## 7. Give Credit Where Credit Is Due

If you are going to include anyone's pictures, work, letters of recommendation—well, anything!—You must first get written permission to do so. If you coauthor any work, get permission from your partners. You might even consider obtaining permission even if you are not sure you are going to include another's work or photo in your digital teaching portfolio. It will save time later on trying to track down the individual and/or the student's parent or guardian. To prevent any misunderstandings and to protect yourself, it is helpful to get permission in writing. In Appendix C, you will find a sample consent form for students and their parents or guardians to sign.

Always make sure to give credit where credit is due. If you know or believe something is copyrighted, then you must provide a reference to the source, and if necessary (depending on the item), get permission to include it in your digital teaching portfolio unless it meets fair use guidelines. In general, we suggest you obtain permission for these items. Some Web sites that have information about copyright include:

- United States Copyright Office, Library of Congress available at http://www.loc.gov/copyright. Also see http://www.loc.gov/copyright/circs/circ1.html for "Copyright Basics" information.
- Educational Multimedia Fair Use Guidelines Development Committee—"Fair Use Guidelines for Multimedia" available at http://www.libraries.psu.edu/mtss/fairuse/guidelinedoc.html.

- University of Texas System, the "Four Factor Fair Use Test" available at http://www.utsystem.edu/ogc/intellectualproperty/copypol2.htm#test. Use the UT system test to see if the material you wish to include in your portfolio meets fair use guidelines.

Some questions to consider when evaluating privacy and copyright are presented in Figure 10.2.

## 8. Protect the Privacy of Your Students and Colleagues

Your privacy is not the only privacy that should concern you. Protecting the identity and privacy of your students and colleagues is just as important. It is good practice to remove the last name of those whose work might be displayed in your digital teaching portfolio. For example, if you plan to share several drafts of a short story written by one of your students (and you have written permission to include the work from the student and the student's parents/guardians) to illustrate your method of scaffolding students through the writing process, it is best to shorten the students' name. Post the student's work with the student's first name only or first name and last initial. In this way, you will be able to make your point without making a students' whereabouts known to the general public.

We also advise teachers to take special care when posting photographs of their students on the Web. Never, and we mean never, post a picture with a student's first and last name. Although we regret that extra caution is necessary in protecting the identity of students and colleagues, it is an essential professional courtesy we must exercise without fail if we care for others.

---

FIGURE 10.2   Questions to Consider About Privacy and Copyright

1. How much (and what) personal information do I want to include in my digital teaching portfolio?
2. Do I want the general public to be able to access all of the information in my portfolio? If not, what information do I want to make available to them? (This will require password protecting some parts of your portfolio.)
3. Do I want to post this information on the Web or just put it on CD?
4. Are all the materials in my portfolio legal?
5. Do I have any copyrighted material in my portfolio?
6. Do I have written consent from colleagues or students' (and their parents) to post their work or digitized photos?
7. Have I removed captions that would connect students or colleagues with their photograph? Have I removed the last names of individuals whose work is displayed in my portfolio?

TABLE 10.4

**Suggested Timeline for Creating Your Digital Teaching Portfolio**

| Week | Activity |
| --- | --- |
| 1 | Read about portfolios, examine examples, determine preliminary table of contents for digital teaching portfolio |
| 2 | Write, share, and revise educational philosophy statement |
| 3 | Review standards, determine theme, begin selecting artifacts, write reflective statements |
| 4 | Continue selecting artifacts that correspond with standards, finalize table of contents for digital teaching portfolio, write reflective statements |
| 5 | Create storyboard of digital teaching portfolio, digitize or convert artifacts that need to be converted to WWW format |
| 6 | Begin actual creation of digital teaching portfolio (creation of Web site, scanning pictures and student work) |
| 7 | Continue development of digital teaching portfolio |
| 8 | Fine-tune reflective statements and design of portfolio |
| 9 | Ask others to critique and evaluate portfolio-in-progress |
| 10 | Make revisions based on critiques; publish, share, and evaluate final digital teaching portfolio |

## 9. Create and Stick to a Timeline

Many of us are procrastinators, but most of us are just plain busy! Your digital teaching portfolio will not get done unless you make the time to create one and make it a priority! And it does take time—time to pull the materials together, and more important, time to reflect on the growth you have experienced as a professional during the time span your work represents. So roll up your sleeves and set some deadlines for your portfolio. Of course, plan in some rewards for meeting these deadlines. Nothing like a little positive reinforcement! See Table 10.4 for a suggested timeline for completing your digital teaching portfolio. We have included writing reflective statements in our timeline. Reflection is an integral part of the digital teaching portfolio development process that will occur throughout the entire process.

It is difficult to say how much time the digital teaching portfolio development process will actually take. Some people spend hours and hours making decisions about the visual appearance of their work (e.g., the background color or pattern for each page). Others wind up reading journals written years ago, skimming all the contents of a unit used during their teaching past, and reminiscing about students to whom they made a difference. It is hard to explain why the simple act of jostling one's memories while going through old files can evoke such powerful memories, but it does! Add technology to the mix, and you have a recipe for being sucked up by your memories and surfing the WWW! So, our recommendations? Be realistic about what you can accomplish and the time you have to achieve what you desire. Then spend some time working toward your goals and reassess them as needed.

## SUMMARY

In this chapter, we provided you with some "commandments" for creating your digital teaching portfolio. These commandments include:

1. When in doubt *don't* throw it out.
2. Do it digital.
3. Be organized, not frustrated.
4. Log it or lose it.
5. If it is nice, save it thrice.
6. Be careful, not sorry. Pay heed to legal and security concerns.
7. Give credit where credit is due.
8. Do unto others as you would have done unto you. Protect the privacy of your students and colleagues.
9. Create and stick to a timeline.

Adhering to these commandments will save you a great deal of time and energy when assembling your digital teaching portfolio. Using these guidelines also will result in a well-organized portfolio and in better relationships with others.

## CHECK YOUR UNDERSTANDING

1. What are some things you should consider before developing your digital teaching portfolio?
2. What are some advantages of saving work, artifacts, and pictures in a digital format?
3. Why is getting consent from other people important?
4. How should files be saved (i.e., format, file names)?

# chapter

# Selecting a
# Design Tool

eleven

The multimedia technologies available today provide teachers many ways to organize and display their work in digital teaching portfolios. Although some teachers find this choice liberating, others find it overwhelming! Regardless, this choice is of great importance as it will influence the portfolio product and the audience that will eventually view it.

This chapter provides an overview of the factors teachers might want to consider when selecting the design tool they will use to create a digital teaching portfolio. We use this term to refer to the various options that you can choose to create your portfolio since the design tools include not only multimedia software programs, but also a simple computer language and Web-based systems that are a hybrid combination of Web applications and software. Included is an overview of some of the most popular design tools, including software, such as The Teacher's Portfolio by Aurbach & Associates and Kid Pix, PowerPoint, HyperStudio, Adobe Acrobat, and

Netscape Composer. Also, we provide a description of a new Web-based software product on the market, the Road e-Portfolio, produced by Chalk & Wire.

# Factors Influencing Design Tool Selection

There are many factors to consider when selecting a design tool for the creation of a digital teaching portfolio.

**AVAILABILITY.**   The first factor deals with design tool availability. Teachers need to decide whether they will use a tool that is already available to them or whether they plan to acquire and use a tool that is not currently available to them. Although many teachers have access to a wide variety of tools in their classrooms, schools, or home, we recognize that this is not always the case. Teachers might need to purchase software or request that their school purchase other tools for them before they can get started creating a digital teaching portfolio. If purchasing software is necessary, other factors may be helpful to consider to make the best decision.

**COST.**   Cost is always a factor worth considering when making important decisions, especially decisions about design tools. Fortunately, many of the tools teachers can use to create digital teaching portfolios are relatively inexpensive or free. Some providers offer special discounts for educators and schools. Other companies, such as Knowledge Adventure, provide free demonstration copies of programs to teachers. We recommend previewing a tool before buying it to determine whether or not it is a good bargain. Many vendors will even allow you to preview the design tool and return it within a certain time period if it does not meet your needs.

**DIFFICULTY.**   Design tools also vary in how difficult they are to learn and use. It is important to keep in mind that the perceived difficulty of a program depends on a person's past experience and current skill set. What may seem difficult to one person may not be to another, and vice versa. Fortunately, most programs we discuss in this chapter are relatively easy to use and are so popular that many teachers already know how to use them. It is helpful for teachers to consider how much time they are willing to invest learning to use a new tool. Time spent on this is often subtracted from the time they can spend attending to the creative aspects of their digital teaching portfolio. If teachers do not know how to use a program, they will want to consider whether they have access to support to help learn or use the program.

**SUPPORT.**   When selecting a design tool for the creation of a digital teaching portfolio, the amount of support available is worth considering. Everyone can benefit from support. Even the most skilled "techies" run into problems that they cannot solve on their own. When selecting tools that friends, colleagues, and school district personnel use, a teacher benefits by being able to get support if it is needed. Some software programs offer extensive manuals, online support, or 1-800 support lines, but not all. Checking the amount of support before making a decision is wise.

**TRANSFERABILITY.**   Time spent learning a tool might be considered a smart investment if skills acquired can be used for some other purpose. We advise teachers to consider the time spent learning to use tools for creating their digital teaching portfolio as time that might help them build skills they can use in their professional or personal activities. For example, some school districts have adopted the practice of requiring students to create portfolios in electronic format. In these situations, teachers working with elementary school students might opt to learn Kid Pix to create their portfolios because it may be the same design tool adopted by their district for the creation of student portfolios. Or, teachers required to teach their students how to create Web sites might have their students create portfolios online.

**SUPPORT FOR VARIOUS MEDIA FORMATS.**   Software programs vary in the support they provide for various media formats. Some design tools let you insert movies, sound recordings, and pictures, whereas others do not. For example, Adobe Acrobat does not support the insertion of multimedia, whereas Kid Pix does. Within design tools that support multimedia there also is variation. Some software support a wider variety of file formats than others. For example, HTML only allows the insertion of three types of graphics files (.gif, .jpg, and .png), whereas PowerPoint supports many more.

**MULTIMEDIA ENVIRONMENTS.**   One of the greatest advantages of creating a digital teaching portfolio is that it fosters a high degree of creativity in the design environment. Teachers may choose a design tool that presents information in a sequential, linear manner that dictates a specific progression through materials. Or, they may select a software program that presents materials in a nonsequential, hyperlinear, manner. Both formats have advantages and disadvantages, but each enables teachers to make creative decisions about how to best present their professional credentials.

**PLATFORM.**   *Platform* is the accepted term used to describe the software operating system and hardware a person is using. At the moment, there are two major platforms, Apple Macintosh/OS and Windows/PC. Although the differences between these platforms are becoming less and less pronounced, these differences can influence decisions about which design tool is best for creating digital teaching portfolios. First off, teachers will want to be sure that the tool they select can run on the computer they plan to use when developing their portfolios. Second, they will want to use a design tool that creates files that can be read on both platforms.

**DISPLAY CAPABILITIES.**   Because the goal for creating any digital teaching portfolio is to display it for others, it is very important to consider the display capabilities of any design tool. The methods used by design tools to save collections of materials vary. Some tools, such as HyperStudio and PowerPoint, have the ability to combine various materials and save them as one file. Other tools, such as Netscape Composer, save files individually. Some design tools require special players in order to be viewed on computers that do not have the program. Some are designed to show materials on the Web. Some tools are perfect to burn files to a CD, whereas others are much better suited to putting files on a Zip disk.

**TECHNICAL REQUIREMENTS.** Because the hardware requirements needed to run various design tools differ, you will want to know the specifications of the computer you will be designing on before you purchase any tools. Information about your processor type (e.g., Pentium, Pentium II, etc.), speed (e.g., mHz), Random Access Memory (RAM), and hard drive space can be compared with the requirements of a particular tool. The requirements for installing and running software usually are found on the side panel of any packaged software program. Most computers can be used to write HTML. See Chapter 12 for more information about hardware.

# Other Factors to Consider when Selecting a Digital Teaching Portfolio Design Tool

**RECOMMENDED STORAGE FORMAT.** Some tools create files that are easier to store and reproduce on the World Wide Web, floppy disk, Zip disk, or CD. The expense associated with different storage devices vary, with the Zip disk being the most expensive (i.e., if you already have access to a CD burner and Web space is free through your school district or educational institution; if not, buying a CD-R or server space might be more expensive than the cost of the average Zip disk).

**AUDIENCE SKILLS REQUIRED FOR VIEWING.** The skill level required for viewing the final digital teaching portfolio is important to consider. Portfolios that are created in files read by programs that many people already own (e.g., Microsoft PowerPoint) and already know how to use (e.g., Netscape Communicator) are preferable. Files created by design tools that require viewers to buy the software program *or* require skills above and beyond the average viewer (e.g., knowledge of how to install a plug-in) will limit potential audiences.

**HARDWARE AND SOFTWARE REQUIREMENTS REQUIRED FOR VIEWING.** Likewise, the technical specifications of the computers your audience will be using to view your files will vary. Teachers should consider the equipment the eventual audience will have access to before creating their digital teaching portfolio. Fancy video and audio files are only useful if they can be accessed quickly and efficiently. Otherwise, these types of files might cause difficulties for audience members with low-end computer systems.

Activity 11.1 provides a brief set of questions you will want to reflect on before choosing which design tool you will use to create your digital teaching portfolio.

## Activity 11.1

### REFLECTING ON YOUR CHOICE OF DESIGN TOOL

Here are some questions to consider when selecting which software you will use to create your digital teaching portfolio:

1. What design tools are available to me at home? At school?
2. At what level are my computer skills? How much am I willing to learn in order to create my digital teaching portfolio? Do I need software at a beginning level, intermediate level? At an advanced level?
3. What type of technical support is available to me? Do I have people in my personal or professional life who can help me if I need help when creating my portfolio? Are there certain design tools that friends or relatives are better able to help me with than others? What programs are the school personnel, colleagues, and other people I know comfortable using?
4. Do I plan to use any design tools I might use to create my portfolio in my teaching?
5. Do I know of any design tools that seem to get good reviews from colleagues who teach courses similar to mine?
6. How important is it that the design tool I use to create my portfolio support files of different types?
7. Do I care whether the design of my portfolio is linear or hyperlinear? Do I care how much creative potential the program has?
8. On what type of computer will those viewing my portfolio try to view it? Mac? PC? Does the design tool I plan to use put information out for both kinds of computers?
9. Do I want to share my materials via the Internet? Does the authoring environment I plan to use support this?
10. How difficult is it to view files created with the design tool I am thinking of using? Will those I want to view my portfolio know how to view it?
11. Can the computer I plan to use in creating my portfolio run the design tool I want to use to create it?

# A Brief Review of Design Tools

There are many design tools you might use to create your digital teaching portfolio. Table 11.1 presents a summary of some of the most popular ones. In the following sections, we will examine these options in detail.

## Kid Pix by The Learning Company

Kid Pix, which is offered by The Learning Company (http://www.learningco.com), has been growing in popularity since the early 1990s because it is a fun, easy-to-use

TABLE 11.1

## Portfolio Design Tool Overview

| Software Program or Authoring Environment | Platform | Ease of Use | Cost | Recommended Storage Format | Creative Capabilities | Presentation Format | Graphic Formats Supported | Video Formats Supported | Audio Formats Supported |
|---|---|---|---|---|---|---|---|---|---|
| Teacher's Portfolio | Mac | Beginner | $195 | Hard drive | Low | Linear/ hyperlinear | .pict | .qt | .aif, .aiff |
| Power Point 2001 | Mac, PC | Beginner | $300 regular edition or $129 academic price | CD, Zip, or Web | Medium | Linear/ hyperlinear | .jpg, .pict, .png, .png, .bmp | .mov, .wmf | .midi, .wav, .mp3 |
| e-Portfolio | Mac, PC | Beginner | $17.50-30.00, depending on volume Free | CD, Web | High | Hyperlinear | .gif, .jpg, .png | .mov, .rm, .ra, .mpeg, .wmf | .wav, .aiff, .midi, most others |
| Netscape Composer | Mac, PC | Advanced | | CD, Zip, or Web | High | Linear/ hyperlinear | .gif, .jpg, .png | .mov, .rm, .ra, .mpeg, .wmf | .wav, .aiff, .midi, most others |
| Hyper Studio v. 3.0 and higher | Mac, PC | Advanced | $199 for teacher's edition | CD, Zip, or Web | High | Linear/ hyperlinear | .jpg, .gif, .pict | .avi, .mov, .mpeg (version 4.0 only) | .wav, .aiff, .mp3 (v. 4.0 only) |
| Kid Pix Deluxe | Mac, PC | Intermediate | $30 | CD, Zip, or Web | Low | Linear | .bmp | .avi, .mov | .avi |
| Adobe Acrobat | Mac, PC | Intermediate | $250 or $60 academic price | CD, Zip, or Web | Low | Linear | Converts graphics in original documents | None | None |

teaching tool that can be used to teach ideas and concepts in all subject areas. Kid Pix provides users a linear, sequential way to present materials. Several versions of the program are on the market, but all have two essential features—one for creating "slides" and one for putting together "slide shows."

Slides might be created using the program's fun but sophisticated drawing tools (stamps, paintbrushes, text tools, etc.) by importing files from another program (photo-editing program, digital camera, etc.), or by using the program's rudimentary animation features. Newer versions of the program support the import of several video file formats. The slide show feature enables the user to sequence individual slides with sounds and transitions. A set of packaged sounds can be chosen or users can record their own with a microphone (provided they are no longer than the 32-second limit).

Kid Pix presentations consist of numerous files of two different types. *Still slides* are saved in two formats—.bmp for PCs and .pict for Mac. *Animations* are saved as .avi files. Slide show files use different storage formats on Mac and PC.

Saving digital teaching portfolios created with Kid Pix is only moderately complicated. A portfolio created in this program will consist of numerous slide files and a slide show file that links them together. The amount of space required for storing the portfolio varies but is based on two factors, the number of slide files used in a portfolio and the size of the slide show. (The size of the slide show is influenced by the number of slide links, the number of transitions, and the number of audio clips included in a slide show.)

Teachers working with students in grades P–5 who consider themselves beginning computers users, have access to the program, and use Kid Pix in their classroom teaching are likely to find this option the most appealing one for digital teaching portfolio creation. Experienced computer users who want more creative choice might find the program's linear presentation format limiting. One major problem with using Kid Pix to create a digital teaching portfolio is that files created with the program cannot be saved and viewed on the Web or by other users unless they own a full version of the software program or download a plug-in. Although this program is relatively inexpensive and widely available, this factor limits the accessibility of portfolios created with this design tool.

## PowerPoint by Microsoft

Microsoft's PowerPoint (http://www.microsoft.com) is a presentation program created for business use but that is found widely in K–12 schools. Many classroom educators have access to the program and use it to enhance student learning opportunities in various subject areas. Workshops that deal with learning and applying this program in educational environments are among the most commonly offered professional development opportunities in school districts. The program is easy to use but has powerful capabilities. It supports many technical features, including hyperlinear design and multimedia objects. In light of these facts, it is not surprising that this program is becoming an increasingly popular creative medium for portfolio creation.

Saving portfolios created with PowerPoint is quite simple. A portfolio created with this program would consist of one slide show file that incorporates various slides containing graphics, sounds, videos, and text. Unlike Kid Pix, PowerPoint slide shows merge all individual slides and related files into one large file that varies in size depending on the amount and type of content in the portfolio. (Slide shows incorporating audio and video require more file space.)

Sharing files created with PowerPoint is relatively easy. Portfolios created with PowerPoint can be saved to floppy disk if they are simple and small. Larger PowerPoint files are best saved on devices with more file capacity, such as Zip disks or CDs. These files can be viewed by anyone who has access to the PowerPoint program (and the program's popularity means that a large number of viewers *do* have this program) *or* a special viewer file can be placed on the disk enabling viewers who do not own the program to view the files. It is worth mentioning that newer versions of the software program have a feature that converts a slide presentation into HTML format when saving the file. This feature enables teachers to make their digital teaching portfolios viewable with a simple Web browser program such as Netscape Communicator either locally (on CD or Zip disk) or globally (if uploaded to a file server on the World Wide Web). You can download the free PowerPoint viewer at http://office.microsoft.com/Downloads.

## HyperStudio by Knowledge Adventure

HyperStudio (http://www.HyperStudio.com) is another popular multimedia program created specifically for use in educational environments. It incorporates many of the same creative features as Kid Pix but enables a hypermedia design. It has many of the same multimedia features as PowerPoint but is more "kid-friendly."

Although the program works much the same as the other options we have discussed, it operates on a card-and-stack metaphor instead of a slide-show metaphor. When using HyperStudio to create a digital teaching portfolio, a teacher first creates a new stack and then creates individual *cards* that incorporate sounds, pictures, video, and transitions. Teachers can create their own media or select media from a gallery included with the program.

Saving portfolios with HyperStudio is easy. The program merges all of the cards in each stack into one file when saving. The size of a HyperStudio files depends on the number of cards in a stack and the types of objects on the cards.

Sharing digital teaching portfolios created with HyperStudio is relatively easy. The portfolio can be shared on a storage device (we recommend Zip disks or CDs) or disseminated via the Web. If files are shared over the Web, the stack file is uploaded directly to a server and linked to a simple HTML document. Those wishing to view the file must have the HyperStudio plug-in, which is available for free on the Internet. The plug-in is available at http://www.hyperstudio.com/downloads/index.html.

## Acrobat by Adobe

Adobe's Acrobat (http://www.adobe.com) offers yet another option for educators who desire to make their professional materials accessible in a digital portfolio format. The program enables teachers to convert any file into Adobe Portable Document Format (PDF). According to Adobe Systems Incorporated (2001), "Adobe PDF is a universal file format that preserves all the fonts, formatting, graphics, and color of any source document, regardless of the application and platform used to create it." By converting files into PDF, practically anyone can view these files using any computer platform because PDF files can be viewed with the free Acrobat Reader, which is available at http://www.adobe.com/products/acrobat/readstep.html.

Using Acrobat for the creation of digital teaching portfolios has many advantages. One is that it translates easily to and from paper portfolios (Barrett 2001) because the formatting of PDF files remains intact, even when printing. Other benefits of using Adobe Acrobat include:

- **Password protection and control access.** You can password-protect PDF documents by requiring a password to access, print, or alter them.
- **Increased readability (accessibility).** To aid those who are motion and vision challenged, you can use the "Make Accessible plug-in" (at http://www.adobe.com/support/downloads) to create PDF files that can be read by a screen reader. The plug-in is available only for Windows 95 or higher machines running Acrobat v. 5 or higher.
- **Digital signatures.** Acrobat allows users to place a digital signature on PDF files. If a file has been altered, the user will be alerted the next time the file is opened.
- **Web-access.** Files converted to PDF format are accessible on the Web using the Adobe Acrobat Reader plug-in.

However, Adobe Acrobat does have its drawbacks. First, the user must own the program, which can be expensive (although education versions are much cheaper). Second, the user needs to learn how to convert and upload files. Third, if distributed on the Web, a reader is needed to access the files. In addition, although the program only allows for the creation of a multilinear portfolio, this feature is quite limited. Also, PDF documents do not support the creativity that can be expressed using other software programs, such as HyperStudio, PowerPoint, or an HTML editing program.

## The Teacher's Portfolio by Aurbach & Associates

Teachers familiar with Aurbach & Associate's (http://www.aurbach.com) Grady Profile (a performance-based portfolio development software program for students of all ages) may find that The Teacher's Portfolio is very similar to it. This is because The Teacher's Portfolio is the educator's version of Grady Profile. Currently, this program is only available for Macintosh and Power Macintosh computers. See http://www.aurbach.com/datasheet_ttp.html for system requirements and a description of the software. The Teacher's Portfolio provides a packaged multimedia format for displaying work. The program allows for the inclusion of sound, graphics, video, and text in portfolios. Each artifact (e.g., sound or video interviews with students or parents; digital photos of bulletin boards, classroom centers, or student projects; the text of lesson plans, etc.) has specific areas for describing the piece, for self-reflection, and for evaluation by the portfolio creator, a supervisor, and a "visitor." The program also has a "notes" section where the portfolio creator can provide additional comments and notes for the viewers.

## Netscape Composer and HTML Editors

HTML is a programming language, not a software program. This language can either be written by hand using a simple text editor (e.g., Word Pad on the PC or SimpleText on the Mac) *or* it can be written with an assistive program called an HTML editing program or Web editor (e.g., Adobe's Go Live, Microsoft FrontPage, or Netscape Composer). When creating a portfolio in HTML, the portfolio files take advantage of the versatility of this design format. Two options exist for files produced in this way—they can be Web-based (created in HTML but stored on CD or disk) or Web-published (created in HTML and put on the Web for all to use).

Producing a digital teaching portfolio in HTML format has a number of advantages. One is that HTML pages can be viewed by anyone who has an Internet connection and a browser whether they are Web-published or merely Web-based. Also, teachers can create links to artifacts that demonstrate or support a particular item in the portfolio or link to other Web sites. For example, one preservice teacher with whom we had worked had studied abroad and added a link in his résumé to the Web site about the program he had attended. Another student created links to the schools where she had completed her student teaching. This could be a powerful tool for an administrator or someone in human resources not familiar with the schools in which the teacher candidate conducted their student teaching or with the programs in which they participated. By creating Web-based or Web-published (HTML) portfolios, teachers demonstrate mastery in using the technologies represented in their Web sites—using graphics, uploading their Web sites to a server, and writing HTML. One student summarized the benefits of using the Web:

> [The digital teaching portfolios] are more interactive, they can be a lot more informational, they are quicker to read, they're easier to access, someone in Missouri can now look at my Web page, they don't have to send a letter to the [Career Services Office] asking to photocopy and send it out.

Another advantage to using HTML as a design tool is that it can possibly help in gaining employment. One preservice teacher reported that he believed he had received two interviews as a result of his digital teaching portfolio, he says:

> I think I've gotten at least two interviews as a result of the electronic portfolio class. One was a model school district in New Jersey and the assistant superintendent specifically mentioned the Internet and going to look at my Web site was what got me the interview. The other one is for a position as the K-to-8 technology director for a private school up in New York. And again it was a result of my experience with the electronic portfolio that the school pursued possible employment with me.

## e-Portfolio by Chalk & Wire

A newer product on the market is Chalk & Wire's Road e-Portfolio (http://www. chalkandwire.com/ePortfolio.htm). Created around suggestions from Professor Deborah Hill at Southern Utah University, Road e-Portfolio is a Web-based system that facilitates teachers' development of digital teaching portfolios in a Web-based format. Individual student licenses can be purchased from Chalk & Wire for $17.50–30.00 depending on the number of teachers using the product in one school or district. The only technical skills required of users are knowing how to use a Web browser and how to navigate the Web site's interface. Visually pleasing, user-friendly wizards automate teachers' uploading of artifacts that demonstrate their competence based on the INTASC standards or any other widely applicable standard that an institution chooses to use as a default. Additional options allow teachers to insert their own standards if they desire.

Teachers use Web-based forms to enter information about themselves and their teaching competence. Teachers can select from many different graphic themes that preselect graphics, colors, and fonts, or they can create and insert their own. The software supports any file types that are Web-compatible, including PDF files, images, and movies. The software itself resides on the Chalk & Wire server and links in the HTML code reference artifact files located on a university's, teacher's, or school district's Web server space. The final portfolio created in HTML format can be downloaded using a program called "Webwhacker" and transferred to CD. The product includes an assessment tool and the ability to distribute one's résumé via the Internet.

Road e-Portfolio and other programs like it provide a simple, low-cost way to put professional materials in digital format. Although the product requires little technical skill to create a digital teaching portfolio, teachers will need technical support to get started and transfer their files to CD. If the objective is to produce a professional teaching portfolio in digital format that can be shared with others in HTML format, this approach offers one of the fastest, most practical methods. This method is recommended when a teacher's time and energy are limited, when teachers have limited interest in developing technical skills, or when teachers do not have the support (e.g., training, incentives) to create a digital teaching portfolio.

## SUMMARY

In this chapter, we explained some of the factors that influence the selection of design tools used for the creation of a digital teaching portfolio. Design tools are languages, software programs, or Web-based tools that can be used to create environments that store portfolio materials. The availability of different design tools in your home and school and the cost of these

tools may influence your selection. The technical knowledge and skill level of the user and the amount of available support for each tool also may be influential. Teachers may want to consider whether specific knowledge and skills can be developed using design tools and could then be applied for other purposes. Some teachers get "double-mileage" when they develop new skills when developing a portfolio and then integrate them with classroom instruction. Design tools vary in the kind of audio, video, and graphic formats they can support. They also vary in the requirements they demand from a user's computer.

## CHECK YOUR UNDERSTANDING

1. Examine the following digital teaching portfolios (or parts of portfolios) created using different design tools, then consider the strengths and weaknesses of each design tool. Consider how the tool influences portfolio design.
   a. HyperStudio: See http://www.Hyper Studio.com/showcase/portfolio.html.
   b. Acrobat: University of Rhode Island has templates on portfolios using Acrobat at http://www.efolio.uri.edu/
   c. Grady Profile: See http://www.aurbach. com/gp2.html. Click on the "demo" link to see a demo link of this software. (This is the actual link, but first you need to complete an info sheet at http:// www.aurbach.com/form_ttpdemo.html.)
2. Download the HyperStudio workbook tutorial at http://www.hyperstudio.com/ library/index.html (look under "Documentation").
3. Try Adobe Acrobat for free by converting a file using "Create PDF Online" at http:// www.adobe.com/products/tryadobe/main. html.

# Hardware and Other Production Tools

The saying "a workman is only as good as his tools" has been around for a long time. This is probably because there is a high degree of truth in the statement. The quality of your digital teaching portfolio will depend both on the quality of the tools you use and how well you use them. In Chapter 11 we discussed some of the different design tools you might choose from to create your portfolio. As you begin to prepare your digital teaching portfolio, you need to be aware of some of the hardware tools that will be required to get the most out of your choice.

Whether you are a regular "Bob Villa" or think that the term "hardware" refers to your diamond engagement ring, you can learn a great deal about the computer hardware and software required for creating a digital teaching portfolio by reading this chapter. We have written it so that it is comprehensive enough to supply advice to those who will be purchasing new equipment for the purpose of creating a portfolio, but it also should be educational for those who are working with "found" equipment in their school or home. As we discuss each type of equipment, we first define its particular function and then explain how it is used in the digital teaching portfolio development process. Next we explain how the product varies in level of quality. Finally, we provide you with some advice about how the choices you make about equipment might influence the production of your digital teaching portfolio.

# Multimedia Computers

Personal computers vary a great deal in this day an age of customization. It used to be that there were only several computer models to choose from, but now it is possible to custom order most features to fit your needs. With more choice comes a greater need for the information required.

The computer you use for the creation of your digital teaching portfolio will be the single most important factor in your personal happiness and professional success through the production end of the portfolio process. The computer's capacity will determine what type of software you will be able to use, how many software programs you will be able to use simultaneously, how much time it will take to do specific tasks, and what type of peripherals (other hardware equipment) will work with your system. Here are just some of the components to consider when purchasing and using a computer to create your digital teaching portfolio.

### RAM

RAM stands for random access memory. RAM is memory that your computer uses for ongoing operations. When you are working at your computer, the computer's microprocessor reads instructions from the keyboard, hard drive, and other components of the system and stores them in RAM. The more RAM you have, the better the performance of the system, because more instructions can be stored and accessed quickly. Generally RAM is expandable. When buying a new computer, buy one that provides space to expand your RAM. The trend in software is that new programs require more RAM. Think of RAM as the short-term memory capacity of your computer. Just like space in your memory—you can never have too much.

RAM is measured in megabytes (MB). Memory comes in increments of 8 or 16 MB. Today's most basic systems are equipped with 16 MB of RAM. You will have the most success with computers containing more than 64 MB of RAM. If your system does not have this amount of RAM, do not worry, as it is fairly easy (and currently inexpensive) to upgrade most machines. It just involves purchasing the right amount and variety of RAM (the variety you need will depend on the brand and model of your machine), opening the machine, grounding yourself to eliminate any excess static electricity (this can be done by standing on a conductive surface connected to the floor and wearing a special wrist-strap or touching an unpainted metal object), and fitting the RAM into a slot in the motherboard. Many computer stores will install extra RAM for you for free if you purchase the RAM from them and provide them with your computer. Increasing RAM in a laptop is more costly and complicated, but it is usually possible.

*Recommendations:* More is better. Memory is cheap now. Buy all you can afford. If you are upgrading, check your owner's manual for the type of memory your computer uses. RAM—not processor speed—is the most important factor in computer performance. Get at least 64 MB of RAM, double that (128 MB) is even better!

## Processor

The processor is the heart of your computer. It determines how fast information is interpreted and communicated within various system components and between peripherals. Processors vary by brand and speed.

**BRAND.**  The Intel Corporation has set the benchmark for the PC processor for the last 15 to 20 years. Although microprocessors created by other competitors such as Advanced Micro Devices (AMD) are becoming more popular, it is tough to beat Intel's record for compatibility with other computer components. Pentium is a brand name of processor from the Intel Corporation. A ranking of processors by generation quality (low to high) is as follows: Celeron, Pentium II, Pentium III, and Athlon.

*Recommendations:* Use the fastest processor you can buy.

**SPEED.**  Processor speed is measured in megaHertz. Current processor speeds range from 100 mHz to more than 700 mHz.. Tomorrow will surely bring even faster speeds. Comparing the speed of different processors can be tricky, as comparisons must be between processors of similar generations.

*Recommendations:* We recommend a minimum of 200 mHz. The speed of this processor will minimize the time you spend waiting to load software files. This will give you more time to learn and be creative.

## Hard Drive

The hard drive, also known as the hard disk, is the most commonly used form of storage. Digital information such as software programs, files, pictures, even digital sound is stored on the hard drive. This information is retained when the computer is turned on and off. One way to think about the hard drive is that it is the long-term memory device for your computer.

*Reccomendations:* When purchasing a hard drive, consider the amount of data it can hold, the rotation speed, access speed, and transfer rate. The greater the amount of space, the better. Hard drives are getting bigger and cheaper every day. Buy the one with the greatest capacity that you can afford at the moment. Disk memory is measured in gigabytes (GB). Get at least 20 GB, but you can double or triple that easily on even a modestly priced machine. If you are planning to create a digital teaching portfolio that will include a large number of video or audio files, be sure to buy an extra large hard drive or some other mass storage device, as these media types require more storage space than pictures and text documents.

## Video System

The video system is used to display moving pictures on your computer. The video system moves information between the video card, the processor, and the system memory.

*Recommendations:* Get at least 8 MB of video memory, which is usually separate from the PC's main memory. If you plan to do much work with digital video, get more than 8 MB.

## Audio System

A computer's audio system consists of speakers and a sound card. In the recent past, sound cards were standard in Apple computers but had to be special-ordered or added later to PCs. The sound card is the output device for all audio information you will access on your computer.

*Recommendations:* Unless you are an audiophile, you will do just fine with a standard sound card and speaker system. If you are interested in recording audio into your computer, you will want to investigate software and audio input equipment such as mixing boards and more sophisticated microphones. You may use your audio system to input voice and music information into your digital teaching portfolio.

## CD-ROM

Over the last couple of years CD-ROM drives have become standard in most personal computers. CD-ROMs are optical media storage devices that can hold over 500 MB of data on a disk that looks like an audio CD. In general, CD-ROM disks are designed for the sole purpose of holding information, so, unlike your hard drive, they cannot be "written to" for the purpose of storing information.

Recently, CD-ROM units that both write and read (and rewrite) have become more affordable. They are called CD-RWs or CD-R. Although they are still more expensive than CD-ROM (read-only memory) drives, they offer the additional advantage of enabling you to store up to 635 MBs of information on a CD. There are various factors to consider when purchasing a CD-ROM recordable or rewritable drive (for more information on CD-RW, see the section later in this chapter). When looking at purchasing a CD-ROM for your computer, you will see that they come in different speeds, such as 2x, 4x, and 24x. These speeds are basically comparisons to the rotation speed of an audio CD.

*Recommendations:* As with other system components, higher numbers indicate higher performance and cost. Most software now comes on a CD-ROM. Without a CD-ROM drive you will miss opportunities to run software that might make a major difference to the development of your digital teaching portfolio.

## Brand

Under the "hood" all PCs are similar, but unless you have some compelling reason not to, we advise sticking with name brands such as Dell and Gateway. The reason? Dependability! Name brand machines tend to be more reliable and provide customer support.

*Recommendations:* We wish we had some for you. We have not found a machine on earth that does not crash, and we have not called a customer support line that dealt with our problems quickly. The best offense is a good defense—buy an extended warranty and extra service agreement if you can afford it. If you do have to use it, you will be glad you invested in it. If you do not have to use it, you will still be happy having some extra security.

## Platform

The term *platform* describes the combination of operating system and computer you are using. There are two primary platforms in existence today: Apple/Macintosh and Windows/PC. In recent years, the operating systems (main computer interface) have begun to resemble one another visually and software interfaces between these platforms have become more compatible. It used to be that files that worked on one platform would not work on another. This has become less of an issue as partnerships between Apple and Microsoft have been forged.

*Recommendations:* If possible, learn to use both computer platforms in your classroom. If you do, you will be better equipped to work with students who use different platforms, and you will be more self-sufficient in any environment. If you cannot learn to work in both platforms, learn the one that is most commonly found in your school, district, or home environment. If buying a new computer, select the platform based on: (1) what you have access to professionally and personally, (2) what people you know and might ask for help use, (3) personal preference, and (4) cost. Most of the software programs that we recommend that you use in the creation of your digital teaching portfolio are available for both platforms.

## Ports and Slots

The ports and slots your computer has will determine what types of peripherals and system extensions you can connect to your computer. Slots are connective areas inside of your computer (located on the motherboard) that allow you to add functionality to your computer when you install expansion cards (e.g., sound cards or video cards). Ports are connective areas outside of your computer that allow you to attach hardware devices called peripherals (e.g., monitors, disk drives, and scanners). Slots and ports vary in their information transfer rates and compatibility with expansion cards and peripherals. Most computers come with the type and number of slots and ports predetermined. Slots commonly found in desktop machines are Industry Standard Architecture (ISA) and Peripheral Component Interconnect (PCI). Cards you install must be compatible with the type of slot your computer has. Popular types of ports include parallel, small computer system interface (SCSI), universal serial bus (USB), and FireWire (also known as the 1394 or I-link). As with slots, the connection on peripherals you wish to use with your computer must be compatible with the type of ports you have. Some ports are unidirectional, meaning they send information only one way. Others are bidirectional and send information both ways.

*Recommendations:* Choose a computer with at least two USB connectors or more. If you plan to add video to your portfolio, consider getting a machine with an even faster port called FireWire. If you are buying a new computer and you already own peripherals and expansion cards that you wish to use with your new system, you will save money if you purchase a computer that is compatible with your existing equipment.

## Monitor

The monitor will influence how you interact with the computer on a regular basis. Several factors, including screen size and dot pitch should be considered when deciding what kind of monitor to buy.

**SCREEN SIZE.**   Monitor screen size is similar to television screen size in that different size displays are available and are measured from corner to diagonal corner. Common monitors start at 14 inches and go up from there. When purchasing a monitor, watch the fine print for the actual viewing area which is slightly less than the actual size of the monitor's cathode ray tube (CRT). This is because the plastic rim, which holds the monitor together, masks a small portion of the CRT.

*Recommendations:* A larger monitor is better to a point. We recommend a 17-inch monitor for best viewing of multiple window applications at the same time, playing games, or surfing the Internet. If you use a monitor that is superior to that which your portfolio audience uses, it can be detrimental. Monitors display information differently based on their size and resolution (amount of information displayed per inch). Information that looks one way on your monitor can look quite different on another, causing many design problems. Using an average size and quality monitor for your design is advisable.

**DOT PITCH.**   Dot pitch describes the size of a pixel. A pixel is the smallest visual unit on a monitor. You have probably noticed pixels without knowing that is what they are called. Pixels are the tiny squares on the computer screen that make up the different graphics, pictures, and text. Although monitors with large dot pitches, up to 0.40 millimeters, are cheaper, their fuzzy screens can cause eyestrain. Look for a monitor with a dot pitch measuring no more than .28 millimeters. This is the one place that smaller is better!

## Modems and ISDN Cards

The modem is the device used by your computer to communicate (usually via telephone line) with the Internet, online services, and other computers. Modems can connect internally throught a slot or externally through a port. Today's multimedia computers contain internal modems as standard equipment. External modems are also available and are often an easy add-on for an older computer.

Modems communicate at a *baud rate,* which communicates how fast the device is capable of sending or receiving data. The early days of data transmission over wire used a rather slow 150 baud rate. This rate was common in the news teletype machines in use into the 1970s. Baud rates have accelerated rapidly in the last couple of years. Early online services used 1400 baud, then 2400. There was a big jump to 14.4k, then 28.8k, 33.6k and now 56k baud modems. Compare today's 56k modem with the early 150 baud modems by converting the 56k to 56,000—the data transfer rate is more than 350 times faster!

A new kind of modem called a *cable modem* enables your computer to take advantage of broadband, or high speed, access in geographic areas where local cable companies have the appropriate equipment. It is important to check with your local cable provider to see if this access is available in your area before buying a cable modem, as such access will not be universal for quite some time. Cable modem access makes using the Internet a more time-efficient, pleasant experience. Cable modems often can be leased from a cable provider. A special fee is required for such access.

Integrated services digital network (ISDN) cards perform the same function as modems and cable modems. They connect computer users to the Internet through fast, broadband access. Data moving through an ISDN card move faster than through a 56k modem. ISDN cards require special telephone lines, which cost a little (or a lot, depending on your phone company) more than normal phone lines.

*Recommendations:* Broadband access is a luxury but not a necessity for most computer novices. If you plan to transfer large files (e.g., video or audio files) for your digital teaching portfolio between your computer and others using the Internet, we recommend a cable modem. It will save you tons of time.

# Scanners

A scanner is a device that records the details of an original document, picture, or other visual object in digital format. Scanners will enable you to digitize (or put in digital format) a variety of artifacts for your digital teaching portfolio, including lesson plans, photographs taken with standard cameras, and student work. There are various kinds of scanners, including flatbed, sheet-fed, photo, and portable scanners. Scanners vary in their resolution, color depth capacity, scan area, port compatibility and dimensions. They come bundled with different amounts and kinds of software.

## Types of Scanners

Flatbed scanners are generally considered the most versatile, as they enable you to scan a range of documents or objects regardless of their size or thickness. Sheet-fed scanners are suitable for scanning single sheets of paper, however, the materials that are scanned need to be detached from the book or magazine. Photo scanners have the ability to scan both 35mm positives and negatives and Advanced Photo System film. These can be scanned as fast as 10 seconds per frame. Portable scanners are also available. They are lightweight and easy to use in different environments, but they tend to be fragile.

*Recommendations:* We recommend that you buy a flatbed scanner due to its versatility and durability. With the variety of materials teachers might include in their digital teaching portfolios, flatbed scanners are most likely to support their needs. Be sure that the scanner you buy is compatible with the ports on your computer, whether Small Computer Systems Interface (SCSI), parallel, USB, or FireWire.

## Resolution

The quality of the scan is determined by the optical resolution the scanner provides. Resolution refers to the sharpness and clarity of an image, represented in dots per inch (dpi). The more dots per inch, the higher the resolution, and the clearer and sharper the scan. For example, 600 dpi means that there are 600 dots across and 600 dots down, so there are 360,000 dots per square inch. Typically, scanners support resolutions from 72 to 600 dpi.

*Recommendations:* When choosing a scanner, your decision should be based on what you plan to scan with the scanner. For basic scanning of most text documents, a 300 dpi resolution is more than enough. The reason? Text documents have a limited amount of information to record. To scan photographs and other objects, a scanner with 800 dpi resolution will do the job. It is important to keep in mind that the resolution of a scanned image is limited not only by the quality of the scanner, but also by the dpi display supported by the output device, that is, your monitor or printer. So even if you scan an image with dpi greater than 300, it will not be visible at this level unless the output device supports dpis of greater than 300.

## Color Depth Capacity

Another factor to consider is the color depth capacity of the scanner, which allows the scanner to distinguish the range of different colors and shades in the documents to be scanned. Each point in an image is called a pixel (short for picture element), and different scanners read the pixels in varying intensities of bits. The greater the bit depth, the more colors or grayscales that can be represented, and the greater the resolution. For example, a 24-bit color scanner can represent $2^{24}$ (16.7 million) colors.

*Recommendations:* The more depth capacity, the better your originals will scan. Buy the best scanner you can afford.

### Scan Area

The scan area is the amount of space that a scanner has for putting materials down. Flatbed scanners vary in the amount of scanning area they allow. This area differs from a postcard size 10 × 15 to 11 × 17 and up.

*Recommendations:* We recommend the largest flatbed scanner you can afford. There is no limit to the size of the materials you might want to scan. We know of one teacher who scanned a poster-sized map her students created in 11 × 17 pieces and put them together using portfolio software.

### Dimensions

The dimensions of the scanner are its physical size measured (usually) in millimeters. The dimensions of a scanner are generally related to its scan area.

*Recommendations:* Make sure you will have enough room on your workstation, desk, or working area to accommodate the scanner. Keep in mind that when you are working on your portfolio you will probably need a lot of surface area to work on because you may have large items you will want to scan.

### Scanner Software

Scanners generally come bundled with software. Almost all come with a software program that connects the scanner to your computer. This software is required to make the two devices work together. Other scanners come with image editing software with which to edit or change images (e.g., adjust the color, size, brightness, etc.) and optical character recognition (OCR) software that lets you scan text documents into your computer as text that can be manipulated versus text that is an image.

*Recommendations:* When constructing your digital teaching portfolio, you will likely require image editing software. Although the versions provided free with scanners are usually scaled-down versions of professional-level software, these programs will get you started. (See the chapter on software for more information.) We also recommend that you select a scanner that comes with OCR software. If you have this handy software, we guarantee you will find a use for it!

# Digital Cameras

Digital cameras record information in digital format rather than on film as conventional cameras do. Once a picture has been taken with a digital camera, it is usually downloaded to a computer system. Then the picture can be manipulated with a graphics program such as Adobe Photoshop. This manipulation often involves resizing the image, changing its file format (e.g., from .pict to .jpg), or altering visual elements.

In the not too distant past, digital cameras and digital video cameras were two separate appliances. Digital cameras stored still photographic information, and digital video cameras stored moving photographic information, as well as audio information. At present, the two types of appliances are becoming more and more similar. Many digital cameras can record short video clips (with or without sound), and most digital video cameras can record still photographic information. Digital photography is one of the most popular and rapidly growing areas of computer technology.

The major factors to consider when selecting a still digital camera are resolution, storage capacity and method, and cost.

Digital cameras have a number of advantages over conventional cameras. Digital cameras enable teachers to capture images for inclusion in their digital teaching portfolios easily, quickly, and inexpensively. Digital cameras are easy to operate because they function much like conventional cameras. Instead of storing information on film, these cameras store information to a storage container such as a disk, CD, cassette, or memory chip. Images from digital cameras can be quickly downloaded to a computer without the wait required for processing and developing film from conventional cameras. In addition, in some ways, digital cameras are less expensive than conventional cameras. Because no film is needed to record information and because development is not required to see the photographs captured by a digital camera, it can be cheaper to operate a digital camera than a conventional one. People often feel that they can take as many pictures as they want with a digital camera because individual pictures do not cost money to produce. However, it should be recognized that digital cameras are often more expensive to purchase than conventional cameras, and the costs associated with printing digital pictures in conventional format can be quite high if special printers or services are used.

However, despite these advantages, digital cameras do present some disadvantages. Unlike film photographs, which have an almost infinite resolution, digital photos are limited by the amount of memory in the camera or storage device used by the camera and the optical resolution of the digitizing mechanism. This often makes digital photography undesirable. The quality of digital images also is influenced by the method used to output the digital image. If a low-end printer is used, pictures often appear grainy and fuzzy, even if they were taken with a digital camera that had a high resolution.

## Resolution

The resolution of digital cameras is usually measured in megapixels (million picture elements). The higher the resolution, the higher quality your image will be provided you have the ability to output it at this level. For more information about the resolution of digital cameras, see http://www.digital-camera-now.com/resolution.html.

## Storage Capacity and Method

Every digital camera must store digital information in order to capture images. How digital cameras store information and how much information they can store varies. Some cameras store images on a 1.44 MB disk, others make use of internal memory chips or portable memory chips, such as the Sony "Memory Stick." Users can make choices based on their own needs and preferences. Digital cameras with internal memory tend to store more information than those that store to disk. Digital cameras also vary in the type of storage cassettes they use.

*Recommendations:* Get the best camera you can afford. You will likely be using it for a long time! If a digital camera is out of your budget right now, we recommend that you consider taking your portfolio pictures with a conventional camera and either scan them into digital format yourself or have a photo developer process them to disk. Many developers now offer this service.

# Digital Video Cameras

When selecting a digital video camera, there are several factors to consider. These include the number of charged couple devices, the image resolution, the number and special features available, the battery life, and the cost.

## Charged Couple Device

The charged couple device (CCD) is the light-sensitive device in most digital cameras that turns the light entering through the lens into electronic signals that can be digitally processed and saved. All but the most expensive cameras have a single CCD, which is the imaging chip in the camera. Most will be quite happy with one CCD, but if you have an unlimited budget, consider cameras with three CCDs, one for each of the three basic colors of a television image: red, green, and blue.

## Special Features

Digital video cameras come with all kinds of features. Here are just a few you may want to look for when considering which camera brand and model to purchase.

- **Special effects.** Some cameras come with the ability to insert special effects filming such as "wipes," "dissolves," "monochrome," and more.
- **Zoom.** Most digital video cameras come with a zoom, but not all work at the same quality. A 10 × optical zoom is sufficient for most, but all zooms should be checked for smoothness.

- **Viewfinder.** Most digital video cameras have a larger liquid crystal display (LCD) panel in addition to a viewfinder. The larger the LCD panel, the better and the more expensive the video camera. Make sure the optical viewfinder is easy to see into, and that it has a flexible rubber boot to block the sun.
- **Image stabilization.** If you have ever operated a video camera, you know it can be difficult to hold the camera still when not using a tripod. Some cameras offer a feature that makes images appear more steady.
- **Battery life.** Battery life also is something to consider. The longer the battery lasts the better!

*Recommendations:* Most will do just fine with a low-end digital video camera. Borrow rather than buy a digital video camera if you can. This type of technology is undergoing many changes that make holding off on a purchase wise!

# Mass Storage Devices

In the last few years, several external storage devices have become popular. The increasing storage space required by software programs and the increasing file sizes that the average user produces have contributed to this trend. The following mass storage devices are used for archiving and back-up purposes as well.

## SCSI Drives

SCSI (small computer systems interface) drives that store information on disks of 100 or 250 MB have been widely adopted by computer users who require more file storage space than a floppy disk provides. Iomega's Zip drive and Jazz drive (see http://www.iomega.com for info on Zip and Jazz drives) provide easy-to-use software that have made these appliances the external storage drives of choice for many computer users.

## CD-RW

CD-Recorders (sometimes called *burners* and CD Reader/Recorder drives or CD-RWs are also mass storage devices. They offer the advantage of having the most universally accepted storage medium—the data compact disk, or CD. The storage capacity of data disks created using these devices is usually 650 MB.

Recent advances in technology have reduced the cost of these devices. CD burners are generally peripherals, or add-ons, that connect to an external port. Data CDs cannot be read by these drives, only recorded. The CD-Reader/Recorder generally comes internal to a computer. It serves the dual purpose of reading (like a standard CD-ROM drive) and recording (like a burner). These devices are more expensive than a burner or a CD-ROM drive on its own because it combines the capabilities of both.

All mass storage drives vary in their dependability, port interface, the speed with which they write information to disk, and the software that comes bundled with them.

## DVD-R

DVD-R (Digital Versatile Disk Recorder) drives can record and read the same types of data found on CD-ROMs. The main difference between DVDs and CD-ROMs is that DVDs can store much more data than CD-ROMs. DVDs were initially created to store video. DVD storage capacity is expressed using a number (e.g., DVD-5 or DVD-9). Storage capacity of DVDs ranges from 4.7 GB (for a DVD-5) to 17 GB (for a DVD-18). If you are planning to create a portfolio with a great deal of video or if you want a mass storage device that will give you lots and lots of growing room you will certainly want to get your hands on a DVD-R drive. The higher the number DVD-R drive you can buy the better. If your expenses are tight, skip this item. At the moment the technology is so new that it is expensive, and because other storage options exist, chances are you can get along without it for now.

*Recommendations:*  If making a choice among existing mass storage drives, put your portfolio on whichever drive is most widely accepted by computer users with whom you would like to share information. If buying a new computer, look for one with a built-in DVD/CD-RW drive, which allows you to create your own CDs.

## SUMMARY

In this chapter, we presented information about the various types of hardware that may be useful when creating a digital teaching portfolio. You will certainly need a multimedia computer to create your portfolio. The features that will contribute to the quality of your experience during the portfolio process include the amount of RAM it contains, the processor speed and brand, and the size of its hard drive.

Other important factors that will influence your experience during the creation of a portfolio are the computer's platform (whether it runs the Windows or Mac OS), its video and audio systems, and CD-ROM drive. Your computer will be useless unless you have a moni-

tor. When selecting a monitor, consider its resolution and dot pitch. Peripheral devices that will be connected to the computer also may be useful and are important to consider. When connecting peripherals to your computer, the type and number of ports on your computer becomes very important. When selecting a scanner, consider its resolution, color capacity, scan area, and the software bundled with it. If you plan to create a large portfolio, you will want to consider various mass storage options. If you have appropriate equipment, creating your portfolio will be easier and much more enjoyable.

## CHECK YOUR UNDERSTANDING

1. Determine what hardware you have available to you. Do you believe it will meet the minimal requirements for you to create a digital teaching portfolio in your chosen format?

2. To learn more about hardware (and software) issues, as well as brief histories of the various technologies, we encourage you to read the "Fast Guides" available in the reference section of Whatis?com available at http://whatis.techtarget.com.

# Principles of Graphic Design

Take a look at the room you are sitting in right now. Chances are, somewhere in this room you will find a piece of media that has been created by one or more professional graphic designers. Maybe this media is a book cover, magazine advertisement, or interface on a computer screen. Regardless of the type of item, the graphic design appearing on this media has been carefully constructed to attract your attention and elicit a certain type of response. Whether you realize it or not, decisions regarding the placement of shapes, colors, text, and other graphics were time-consuming, deliberate, and based on basic principles of graphic design. In this chapter, we provide you with an opportunity to consider the importance of graphic design and the potential effects that graphic design can have on your digital teaching portfolio. We will provide a brief overview of the principles of graphic design and make some suggestions for how you can apply these principles to create a portfolio that will entice your viewer and communicate important elements of your personality and professionalism.

# The Importance of Graphic Design

Although most of us know that "you can't judge a book by its cover," most of us have probably made a choice based on visual appeal at one time or another. Regardless of whether it is an effective strategy or not, people tend to form fast and firm opinions of things based on how they look and appear. Visual effects are most commonly used to entice. Those working in the restaurant industry take advantage of the human proclivity to yearn for food that looks good—often before we know anything about its taste! Who can pass up a dessert tray when it moves past the table, laden with goodies? Let's admit it, we have all fallen for that trick willingly!

However, visual appearance also can influence people in negative ways. If visual effects can be enticing, they also can be repellant! Indeed, certain colors and shapes have the power to turn people off. Which of us would respond well to a Web page with a blood-red background? Or, what about a wallpaper with a radiating black and white design? Reaction to visual design is often a matter of personal preference. Personal preference often is affected by a combination of experiences, environmental conditioning, and culture.

It is interesting to consider that our taste for visual design is just as much a product of our culture as our culinary taste. Awareness of the fact that various colors and shapes and combinations have specific cultural connotations keeps designers from offending others unintentionally. Although it is quite difficult to know all information about cultural responses to color and design, being open and making an effort to be culturally sensitive is the right approach for building positive relationships.

Negative reactions to graphic designs are not only a result of cultural preferences. Some problems transcend the boundaries of culture! Designs that include too many visual elements or display these elements in a disorganized fashion are offensive to people of *all* backgrounds. Dull designs, those that do not use the principles of graphic design effectively, failing to evoke *any* reaction from a viewer, can be just as bad.

# The Principles of Graphic Design

The four principles of graphic design are contrast, repetition, alignment, and proximity. As you develop your digital teaching portfolio, you will need to consider the application of these principles to both individual pages in your portfolio and to the portfolio design as a whole. Doing this will help you to create a portfolio that has visual continuity (almost as important as the other type of continuity we discussed in Chapter 5).

To illustrate the application of these principles to an individual page in a portfolio, imagine the page containing the table of contents of your portfolio. On this page (or slide), you have what we will call *graphic elements*. Graphic elements consist of any item on a page that becomes a visual unit. A line of text, a picture, a color, and a horizontal line are each examples of graphic elements. To apply appropriate contrast, you manipulate the graphic elements that make up the titles for each area of your portfolio by using different colors. On a page with a white background, you type "Professional Credentials" in navy blue, "Standard 1" in forest green, "Standard 2" in burgundy, "Standard 3" in purple, "Standard 4" in gun-metal gray, and "Personal Information" in black. To apply *repetition,* you choose to use the same two fonts (12 pt. Times New Roman for the titles and 10 pt. Arial for description text) on the entire page. To make use of *alignment,* you place the graphic elements of text and shapes on the page to achieve visual balance (aligning the text to the center, left, or right). To apply the principle of *proximity,* you will want to make sure that items that are similar are grouped together. This means that you put the descriptions for each title right below the title. See Figure 13.1 for an example of a table of contents using these conventions.

To illustrate the application of these principles throughout your entire portfolio, imagine the many pages of your portfolio. To apply contrast, you carry through the color contrast you began on your table of contents page by using different colors for the titles in each portfolio area. You place the title for pages in each section at the top of each page in the same color it appeared on the table of contents page. Therefore, at the top of every page demonstrating "Standard 1," the title appears in forest green. See Figure 13.2 for an example of this method. The contrast is applied because the pages in every section appear very different from one another and can be differentiated visually. By placing the same title in the same color on every page

### Wilma I. Ball

**digital teaching portfolio**

**Professional Credentials**- information about my professional preparation and professional development.

**Standard 4** - my philosophy of education and beliefs about teaching, learning and education as a profession.

**Standard 2**- examples of lesson plans and other instructional materials.

**Standard 3**- see examples of my work on evaluation and assessment.

**Standard 4**- learn about my ability to communicate with parents, students and other colleagues.

**Personal Information**- find out more about what I do when I'm not teaching

FIGURE 13.1 Table of Contents Example

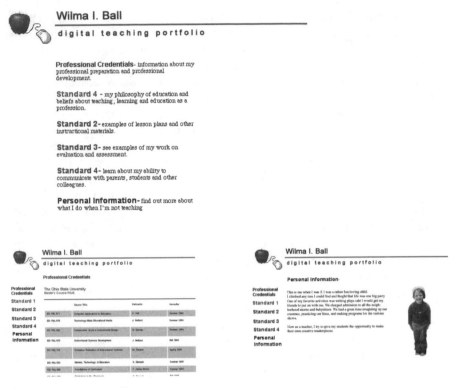

**FIGURE 13.2**　Effective Repetition

in each individual section, you are applying the principle of repetition. Applying repetition creates continuity between all of the pages in a particular section. Because of repetition, all of the pages in the area on "Professional Standards" look alike. You also can apply repetition by repeating the same fonts and sizes for the titles of each section consistently throughout your entire Web site. To the greatest extent possible, each page in your portfolio should be aligned the same way. The pages in the section on "Standard 1" should line up pictures and text with the same alignment scheme as the pages in the section on "Standard 2." Proximity is applied by grouping all the information about "Standard 2" with pages about Standard 2 and grouping all the pages about "Professional Information" with other pages about professional information. If these things seem common sense to you, good! Then you have already picked up some important lessons about graphic design just by viewing other pages with good graphic design!

## Contrast

Contrast is created when two or more graphic elements are very different from one another. To use this principle properly, you will want to avoid elements (font, size, colors, shape, space, etc.) that are similar. Either make them the same or make them very different.

The most important contrast required in a design is the contrast between the text color and the background color. The color of the text and the background need to be very different from each other in order to be read with ease. It would not work very well if you had a page with white text and a pale blue background would it? Nor would it work well to have a page with a black background and navy blue text. Many different color combinations will work, but as a rule of thumb, you should have at least 80 percent contrast between the foreground and background. If you are not good at determining percentages, just ask yourself this simple question. Do you have to struggle to read the page? If the answer is yes, you probably need more contrast. To practice applying appropriate background and text colors, try Activity 13.1.

## Activity 13.1

### BACKGROUND SELECTOR

1. Go to the following Web site: http://www.imagitek.com/bcs.html.
2. When you get to this page, you will be able to select different text and background colors to see how they work together.
3. Decide which combination of colors contrasts best.

We want to stress that color is only one graphic element that can create contrast. Size is another graphic element that may be used to create contrast. Using very large and very small text or very large pictures (e.g., a logo) and very small pictures (e.g., thumbnails or small renditions of student work) also can create contrast. Font style is another way to create contrast. You might use two different font types—one very serious, such as Times New Roman, and another, rather flippant one, such as Jokerman to create a contrast between pages that include student work and a teacher's work or between professional work and a teacher's personal interests.

We share one cautionary message to those trying to create contrast by using different fonts. Be aware that fonts can be problematic when sharing portfolios with individuals who are using different types of computers. Many fonts come only with certain programs. In these cases, a font that you have on your machine and use in your portfolio may not be present on another machine. When your portfolio is viewed by this person, the next closest font they do have will be substituted for the font that you used, and they will not get the same visual effect you intended. To be safe, stick to fonts that are fairly common or put the font in a graphic. Here is a list of common fonts:

- Arial
- Geneva
- Helvetica
- Times

FIGURE 13.3    Effective Contrast

- Times New Roman
- Verdana

Other types of contrast can be equally effective. We encourage you to experiment and discover these methods on your own.

*Ideas for Applying Contrast in a Digital Teaching Portfolio Page or Slide*

- Use contrasting text and background colors.
- Use different fonts for titles and body text.
- Have very serious-looking graphic elements next to very fun-looking graphic elements.

*Ideas for Using Contrast in an Entire Digital Teaching Portfolio*

- Pages for certain sections might have a different colored background.
- Title text might be very different for different sections.
- Pages with student work might look very "juvenile," and those for adult work and reflection might look very "grown-up." Create this effect with color, alignment, and font.

For an example of the effective use of contrast, see Figure 13.3. For an example of ineffective contrast, see Figure 13.4.

## Repetition

Repetition is created by continued use of a particular visual element (i.e., font, size, color, texture, space, etc.). Repetition creates a sense of unity and consistency in a

Welcome to
*Wilma I. Ball's Portfolio*

-**about me**
-**my philosophy**
-**sample lesson plans**
-**technology metaphors**
-**mindtools**

FIGURE 13.4  Ineffective Contrast

graphic design. It also helps to organize a design, making it easier for the viewer to interpret and experience.

You can repeat many different graphic elements on each page and on a series of pages in your digital teaching portfolio. Fonts (e.g., Times, Arial, etc.), styles (e.g., bold, italic, etc.) colors, alignment, and other visual elements such as page background colors and textures, lines, and logos can all be repeated. It is important to take special care to repeat the same variation of each element when you repeat it. For example, if your title text for each page is in "18 pt., Times, bold, green" then repeat it this way every time you type the title. We recommend using the edit features (cut, copy, paste) whenever possible. Cutting and pasting elements you want to repeat can ensure that they are consistent in every detail and save extra time and energy.

Repetition is something that most teachers know very well. Think of how many times you have to tell students to quiet down in the classroom! As silly as it may seem, there can be a great deal of comfort in repetition. Most people like to hear a favorite story over and over again. However, it is important to keep in mind that repetition of something that is unpleasant can be quite painful! Before you repeat an element in your graphic design, you will want to make sure that it works. For example, if you plan to use a common graphic on every page in your digital teaching portfolio (e.g., a logo with an apple and your name on it), show it to people and see what they think of it before you take the time and energy to repeat it throughout your portfolio.

*Ideas for Applying Repetition in a Digital Teaching Portfolio Page or Slide*

- Repeat the same font throughout the page/slide.
- Repeat the colors in different graphics on different places in the page/slide.
- Repeat the same spacing for text groupings.

*Ideas for Using Repetition in an Entire Digital Teaching Portfolio or Slide*

■ Repeat a logo or banner graphic on the top of every page/slide.
■ Repeat the menu in the same place on every page/slide.
■ Repeat link or other type colors and size on every page/slide.
■ Repeat the same textured background on each page/slide.

For more on applying repetition to a digital teaching portfolio, see Activity 13.2, for an example of repetition, see Figure 13.2.

## Activity 13.2

### REPETITION

1. Take some time to explore the clip art collection you have available in the software program you have chosen to use for creating your portfolio.
2. Look to see if you can find any pictures that might be suitable for use as a logo or banner graphic. These designs will be repeated throughout your portfolio. Resist the temptation to use many different graphics in your portfolio, and just stick to one simple recurring graphic.
3. Consider including your name near this logo on every page in the same style of font.

## Alignment

Alignment refers to the placement of elements on a page. The placement of graphic elements should always be intentional. Decisions about where to position elements on a page should be based on a desire to make a page look interesting rather than to just fill up space. Graphic elements can be aligned to the left, right, center, top, or bottom of a page.

When you squint to look at a page, you will notice that there is a visual connection between graphic elements appearing on a page. This connection is sometimes called *page flow*. Elements that are grouped together so that they facilitate this flow will be more easily viewed by others. Elements that are grouped so that they interrupt this flow will get the viewer's attention. Good designers use this information to their advantage.

Figures 13.5 and 13.6 show examples of the effective and ineffective use of alignment. Look at the graphics with your eyes squinted. Notice that in Figure 13.5, the elements on the page flow smoothly and that, in Figure 13.6, they appear choppy and out of order.

*Ideas for Applying Alignment in a Digital Teaching Portfolio Page or Slide*

■ Align the elements in your table of contents either center, left, or right.
■ Align the logo at the top of the page so that it compliments the other graphic elements on the page/slide.

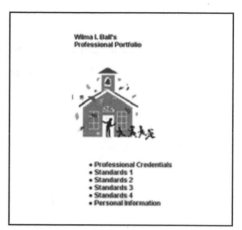

FIGURE 13.5  Effective Alignment  FIGURE 13.6  Ineffective Alignment.

*Ideas for Using Alignment in an Entire Digital Teaching Portfolio*

■ Use the same alignment scheme for each page/slide.
■ Put the menu or table of contents for portfolio in the center at the bottom of every page/slide.

## Proximity

The principle of proximity dictates that you group graphic elements that are related close to one another. This grouping contributes to the organization of information for both the eye and the mind. The principle also dictates that you group unlike graphic elements apart from one another. This keeps these elements from getting confused with one another on the page and in the mind of the viewer.

Proximity can be applied to pages by grouping information that is related close together. Before designers can put information in this order, they must first know what information should be grouped together. This requires a thorough review of information that will be included before designing a page. Pointers on how to group and organize information are covered in Chapter 7.

Proximity also is important to apply to a digital teaching portfolio as a whole. This may be accomplished by examining how the elements on each page are balanced. Use the following suggestions to incorporate the principle of proximity in your portfolio.

*Ideas for Applying Proximity in a Digital Teaching Portfolio Page or Slide*

■ Information about individual topics and descriptions of these topics are grouped together.

- Information that identifies the creator of the page, grade level taught, and school of employment are grouped together.
- The menu with links to various sections of the page appears in close proximity.

*Ideas for Using Proximity in an Entire Digital Teaching Portfolio*

- All student work is grouped together in one area of the portfolio.
- Professional credentials such as teaching certificates, graduate transcripts, etc. are grouped together.
- Work that demonstrates individual curriculum standards is grouped together.

# Factors that Might Affect the Visual Appearance of Your Digital Teaching Portfolio

There are some factors that might affect the visual appearance of your digital teaching portfolio are things over which you have no control. The following factors may affect how your portfolio appears.

- **Browser's font and font size.** As mentioned previously, if the person viewing your portfolio does not have the particular font that you used in creating your digital teaching portfolio, then this person's computer will use a default font such as Arial or Times New Roman to display text. This can affect alignment of text and other elements.
- **Monitor resolution.** If you read Chapter 12, then you know that different monitor resolutions can affect what your portfolio looks like on the screen.
- **Web site designer's specifications for font and font size.** If a Web site was created to display the portfolio, then you can specify the use of particular fonts, even if a viewer has set certain fonts and sizes in the preferences section of their browser (Williams and Tollet 2000, p. 226).

## SUMMARY

In this chapter, we explained some of the reasons why graphic design is such an important part of your digital teaching portfolio. The principles of graphic design, if applied appropriately, can enhance your portfolio and communicate your professionalism. The principles of graphic design include contrast, repetition, alignment, and proximity. Application of these principles should be made to individual portfolio pages (or slides) and the entire portfolio. Incorporating these principles in the development of your portfolio will help you to create a visually pleasing portfolio. Finally, keep in mind that the people who view your portfolio will have equipment that may or may not be able to display your portfolio exactly as you designed it. For example, the fonts available on other's computers might be different from the ones available on yours.

## CHECK YOUR UNDERSTANDING

1. Examine the following Web sites:
   a. Cooper Hewitt National Design Museum available at http://www.si.edu/ndm/dfl/dflhome.htm
   b. The Valley of the Shadow available at http://jefferson.village.virginia.edu/vshadow2/reception.html
   c. The Guggenheim's "The Art of the Motorcycle" available at http://www.guggenheim.com/lowb/visarts/exhibitions/motorcycle/flash5.html (requires Flash viewer)

   How did these sites incorporate the principles of alignment, contrast, proximity, and repetition?
2. What are graphic elements?

# epilogue

In this book, we have shared with you what we know about digital teaching portfolios. We have explained what they are and described approaches for developing them. We also have shared with you some of the ways digital teaching portfolios can benefit educators.

In this epilogue, we want to reiterate that there is no one right way to create a digital teaching portfolio. The processes and activities presented in this book represent some successful methods that we have used to help teachers develop portfolios. Many of the processes should be repeated over and over again—not just once in succession!

As you create a digital teaching portfolio, you will embark on an important educational journey. This journey will require a great deal of energy, reflection, learning, and relearning. It will make you feel both frustrated and satisfied. This journey will unite your past, present, and future learning experiences. It will require you to reflect on what you have learned, make you question what you know, and push you to consider what you need to learn to grow as an educator. As you make this journey, remember that you do not have to travel alone. Although the process of creating a digital teaching portfolio is presented as one that is individual, it also can be communal. Activities need not be individual, they can be collegial. We challenge you to consider ways to share the digital teaching portfolio process with others.

# The Principal's Digital Portfolio

Why would a principal create a digital portfolio? There are several reasons. Digital portfolios help showcase principals' knowledge, leadership, and technology competence, support teaching portfolio initiatives, and teach principals about themselves and their practice.

However, before we explain the benefits, we first need to define what a principal's digital portfolio is. According to Brown and Irby (2001), a principal portfolio "is a collection of thoughtfully selected exhibits or artifacts and reflections indicative of an individual's experiences and ability to lead and of the individual's progress toward and/or attainment of established goals or criteria" (p. 2). They also suggest that there are three types of principal portfolios: professional development, evaluation, and career advancement. Each of these portfolios has different purposes and audiences. See Table A.1 for an outline of the purpose, audience, and benefits of each of these portfolios. The principal's digital portfolio contains all of the same elements found in the principal portfolio, but, like a digital teaching portfolio, it is presented in a digital format.

## Artifact Possibilities for Principals

Although some of the artifacts present in a principal's digital portfolio are the same as those in a teacher's, there are several artifacts that are very different because a principal's job is different from a teacher's. Principal portfolios should reflect leadership, organization, and management skills. Some artifacts that might be included are the principal's leadership philosophy, educational philosophy, short- and long-

TABLE A.1

**Types of Principal Portfolios**

| Type | Purpose | Audience | Advantages |
|------|---------|----------|------------|
| Professional growth (working portolio) | Self-evaluation | Self, peers | Serves as a catalyst for change and self-reflection |
| Evaluation (presentation portfolio) | Summative evaluation | Self, principal's supervisor, peers | Individualized approach to assessment |
| Career advancement (presentation portfolio) | Secure employment or advancement opportunites | Principal's supervisor, interviewing committee | Offer evidence of leadership skills and experience |

*Source:* Brown and Irby (2001).

term goals, staff development plans, personal development plan, letters of appreciation, budgets, meeting agendas, résumé, videotapes, case studies, newsletters, memos, parent and teacher evaluations, information from meetings, principal performance reviews, and materials from parent and teacher conferences.

# Benefits of Digital Principal Portfolios for Principals

## Portfolios Enable Leading by Example.

Some principals have discovered the value of leading by example. If principals are planning to advocate the use of digital portfolios with teachers and/or students, they can gain a great deal by participating in the process themselves. Like teachers, principals can collect artifacts demonstrating their professional competence and display them in a digital dossier. Artifacts might be selected to demonstrate effective communication (e.g., newsletters, memos, press releases), instructional leadership (e.g., faculty meeting presentations on new educational ideas, photos of school assemblies, and diagnoses of cumulative student performance such as proficiency test scores), and support of faculty (e.g., jointly crafted faculty development plans, e-mail messages, and teaching evaluations).

When principals reflect on their work and select samples from it for inclusion in their professional portfolios, they begin to recognize areas of strength and weakness. If they use this knowledge to chart their own professional growth, they can become better leaders.

Like teachers, principals can find the process of compiling their work to be rewarding, as it produces tangible evidence of their professional efforts. They can experience a great sense of personal satisfaction and increased self-esteem. Also, a principal's digital portfolios serve as an excellent public relations tool. In addition to experiencing many of the professional benefits teachers experience, principals who create their own digital portfolios often find that they become more influential school leaders.

## Principal Involvement Supports the Portfolio Initiative

Prin-cipals who "practice what they preach" and create their own digital portfolios gain credibility in the eyes of their faculty. Teachers—whether they have already bought into the portfolio process or not—will likely enter the venture with enthusiasm if they know that their school leader believes it is important enough to try. For example, one principal we know volunteered to participate in a district-wide pilot project to create portfolios. As a result, she received publicity throughout the school district and city for being an innovator in this area. When the time came for the teachers in this principal's school to create their own portfolios, they knew that their leader's reputation was on the line and gave their best efforts when it was their turn to participate.

The involvement of principals in creating digital portfolios can facilitate their efforts to promote the process by providing them information that can influence decision making about portfolios. When principals experience the challenges and benefits of the process for themselves, they can incorporate this knowledge into efforts to influence their staff. For example, if a principal uses a particular computer in the teacher workroom to create his or her portfolio, the principal is more likely to discover if the hardware's technical specifications facilitate or hinder the process. This first-hand discovery of the potential challenges might alleviate the loss of time teachers will experience if they discover this themselves. Principals creating their own portfolios can discover many other bits of important information as well.

## Portfolio Development Demonstrates Competence Related to Standards.

The standards movement has not left school leaders untouched. Principals should consider creating their portfolios to respond to national standards to demonstrate their competence. National groups such as the American Association for School Administrators (http://www.aasa.org), the National Policy Board for Educational Administration (http://www.npbea.org), and state departments of education provide listings of professional competencies that could make excellent organizational frameworks for a principal's digital portfolio.

Principals might also consider developing portfolios using the Interstate School Leaders Licensure Consortium's (ISLLC) NCATE-compatible model standards for school leaders (http://www.ccsso.org/isllc1.html). These standards represent a common core of knowledge, disposition, and performances for school leaders to link effective leadership with improved educational outcomes. The Council of Chief State School Officers (http://www.ccsso.org) guided the creation of the consortium, which is composed of 32 education agencies and 13 education administrative associations. The ISLLC standards (1996) state that a school leader is an educational leader who promotes the success of all students by:

- Facilitating the development, articulation, implementation, and stewardship of a vision of learning that is shared and supported by the school community.
- Advocating, nurturing, and sustaining a school culture and instructional program conducive to student learning and staff professional growth.
- Ensuring management of the organization, operations, and resources for a safe, efficient, and effective learning environment.
- Collaborating with families and community members, responding to diverse community interests and needs, and mobilizing community resources.
- Acting with integrity, fairness, and in an ethical manner.
- Understanding, responding to, and influencing the larger political, social, economic, legal, and cultural context.

Several states that are part of ISLLC have been collaborating with the Educational Testing Service (ETS) to develop a portfolio assessment for school leaders based on the ISLLC Standards. Some of these states will likely use the portfolio assessment for licensure and/or licensure renewal. Therefore, many principals will have to create some type of portfolio anyway—Why not a digital one?

Also, principals interested in demonstrating technical competency might decide to respond to the technology standards issued by the Collaborative for Technology Standards for School Administrators (TSSA 2001) (http://www.ncrtec.org/pd/tssa). The TSSA Collaborative has developed national technology standards for school administrators. The TSSA members are from professional organizations, state departments of education, and business. The "Technology Standards for School Administrators" (TSSA 2001) are:

1. **Leadership and Vision.** Educational leaders inspire the development of a shared vision for comprehensive integration of technology and foster an environment and culture conducive to the realization of that vision.
2. **Learning and Teaching.** Educational leaders ensure that curricular design, instructional strategies, and learning environments integrate appropriate technologies to maximize learning and teaching.
3. **Productivity and Professional Practice.** Educational leaders apply technology to enhance their professional practice and to increase their own productivity and that of others.
4. **Support, Management, and Operations.** Educational leaders ensure the integration of technology to support productive systems for learning and administration.
5. **Assessment and Evaluation.** Educational leaders use technology to plan and implement comprehensive systems of effective assessment and evaluation.

6. **Social, Legal, and Ethical Issues.** Educational leaders understand the social, legal, and ethical issues related to technology and model responsible decision making related to these issues.

## Portfolios Teach Principals

As decision makers, principals require a great deal of knowledge to do their jobs. Knowledge about curriculum, instruction, assessment, psychology, home–school relations, organizational change, and more factor into their everyday interactions on the job. Creating portfolios can provide principals with a way to take stock of what they already know and what they need to know. In this way, they can identify areas of strength and weakness around which they can focus their future growth.

Two knowledge areas in which many principals require development are technology and authentic assessment. The creation of a portfolio in digital format can provide principals a much-needed venue for developing knowledge and skills in these areas. When engaging in the development of a digital portfolio, principals have the foremost opportunity to develop basic technology skills and knowledge of the authentic assessment process. If appropriately applied, this knowledge can contribute to their increased ability to make decisions that influence students and teachers alike.

# Digital Teaching Portfolio-Centered Professional Development: A Plan for Helping School Districts Deal with Problems Related to Professional Development

There are many positive outcomes resulting from high-quality, career-long professional development, including increased collegiality, improved content-area knowledge, retention, and vitality. Career-long professional development has been found to contribute significantly to the retention and continued vitality of teachers. Although professional development is recognized as important to educational quality, little innovation exists in this area. Traditional models of professional development—namely graduate-level courses and workshops (offered by districts or private providers)—are still the predominant means by which teachers learn on the job. Several problems contribute to the failure of most professional development opportunities.

## Problems with Time

Professional development poses at least three problems related to time. First, teachers do not have enough time to spend doing professional development. The work teachers perform, because it is so important, is very time-consuming. To perform their jobs well, teachers must keep current with the curriculum, manage paperwork related to student performance, and contribute to the life of their school by serving on committees and a variety of other time-consuming tasks. Professional development requires additional time beyond this, and realistically, it is not always available.

The second problem related to time is that professional development opportunities are rarely offered at times convenient for teachers. Workshops and classes scheduled at the end of the school day often interfere with other events of equal importance to teachers—namely meals, children's activities, and other personal pursuits. Because teachers' workdays often begin early in the morning and can be physically, emotionally, and intellectually exhausting, professional development opportunities offered in the evening are particularly challenging for teachers.

The last problem related to time is that professional development is not an efficient use of time for teachers. Usually, a good percentage of what is dealt with in professional development offered by third-parties does not have any direct relationship to the problems and concerns teachers are dealing with at a given moment.

# Problems with Travel

To take advantage of professional development opportunities, teachers are often required to travel from their place of work to some other location. Whether to an off-campus graduate education center or a district training facility, travel to attend classes or workshops consumes time that might be spent more productively. Travel is not only time-consuming, it also is costly. With teachers' salaries being what they are, professional development that requires travel is often cost-prohibitive.

# Problems with Transfer

Research on professional development has indicated that teachers often have difficulty transferring what they learn in professional development opportunities into their work in classrooms.

The reason we point out some of these problems with traditional professional development is because the process of creating a digital teaching portfolio can provide teachers a professional development opportunity that overcomes such problems. The creation of digital teaching portfolios can result in better transfer of learning because teachers can apply many of the skills learned in developing a portfolio to classroom practice through the application of technology or portfolio assessment of students.

# Addressing the Problems with Time

The process of creating a digital teaching portfolio is responsive to the multiple problems of dealing with limited time. Although creating a portfolio admittedly takes a great deal of time, the time spent on this task can be spent at a teacher's discretion. Teachers can work on their portfolios any time of day or night. They can decide how much time to spend on each component of their portfolio based on their individual needs and interests. For example, a teacher may decide to spend a great deal of time selecting representative artifacts or reflecting on his work. Or, the same teacher may choose to devote many hours to designing a theme and electronic graphics to support that theme. The decisions that teachers make about the allocation of time and energy also can be based on how they believe their professional development time is best spent.

# Addressing the Problems with Travel

Creating a digital teaching portfolio does not require teachers to travel, as most of the materials that will be required are in fact close at hand. Artifacts will most likely be stored in teachers' classrooms, basements, car trunks, or closets. Some travel may be necessary if teachers must travel to seek assistance from others.

# Addressing the Problems with Transfer

If teachers make wise decisions about how to focus their time and energy during the digital teaching portfolio creation process, they can use this time to develop skills and knowledge that will transfer both directly and indirectly to their classroom practice. For example, teachers who want to involve their students in creating multimedia presentations probably would apply what they have learned about the program PowerPoint when they teach their classes to use the program. Or, if teachers experience difficulties with various aspects of instruction, they might identify areas of weakness by reflecting on the lesson plans they decide to include in their portfolios and strategize ways these problems might be avoided in the future.

However, it would be unrealistic to think that all transfer could occur without additional help. We suggest that teachers work in supportive groups to create their digital teaching portfolios. If groups are structured appropriately, the members can pool their resources and benefit from collective knowledge and skills. More experienced teachers might share their professional insight about assessment, behavior management, and curriculum planning, whereas less experienced teachers might provide fresh perspectives on instruction and the application of technology.

The U.S. Department of Education has identified a number of characteristics of high-quality professional development. These are presented in Figure B.1.

FIGURE B.1

▬▬▬▬▬

## Characteristics of High-Quality Professional Development

The mission of professional development is to prepare and support educators to help all students achieve to high standards of learning and development. It does the following:

- Focuses on teachers as central to student learning, yet includes all other members of the school community:
- Focuses on individual, collegial, and and organizational improvement;
- Respects and nurtures the intellectual and leadership capacity of teachers, principals, and others in the school community;
- Reflects best available research and practice in teaching, learning and leadership;
- Enables teachers to develop further expertise in subject content, teaching strategies, uses of technologies, and other essential elements in teaching to high standards;
- Promotes continuous inquiry and improvement embedded in the daily life of schools;
- Is planned collaboratively by those who will participate in and facilitate that development;
- Requires substantial time and other resources;
- Is driven by a coherent long-term plan;
- Is evaluated ultimately on the basis of its impact on teacher effectiveness and student learning; and this assessment guides subsequent professional development efforts.

*Source:* U.S. Department of Education (2000).

# Letter to Parent/Guardian Describing Release Form

Date: _____

Dear Parent/Guardian:

    I am creating a Web-based Digital Teaching Portfolio. My digital teaching portfolio contains a variety of materials such as curricular units, writing samples, and evaluations of my teaching. As part of my portfolio, I would like to include photos and samples of student work to demonstrate my teaching experience. Your child's name will not appear anywhere in my portfolio. If you agree to have your child's work displayed in my portfolio, please sign and return the release form enclosed in this envelope.

Sincerely,

_____
Your name here

# Minor Release Form

I give permission for <u>insert your name here</u> to utilize my minor child's, <u>insert child's name here</u>, image/work and to reproduce materials in my digital teaching portfolio that will be posted on the World Wide Web that my child has produced as a result of classroom activities. As a condition of my child's participation, I understand and agree that:

1. I am to receive no compensation for this participation;
2. My child's image or work confers upon me no ownership rights of any kind, including but not limited to my rights in copyright,
3. The materials produced may be used for educational purposes, and
4. My child's name will not be connected with any images or work.

I hereby release you from any liability for claims of any kind whatsoever arising out of my child's participation in the production of, or appearance in, the educational materials.

_____        _____
Signature, Parent or Guardian                    Date


_____
Name Printed


_____        _____
                                                                Phone Number

_____


_____
Permanent Address
(or address/phone of someone who will always be able to reach you)

# references

Adobe Systems Incorporated. (2002). *Adobe PDF*. Retrieved January 29, 2002, from http://www.adobe.com/products/acrobat/adobepdf.html

Alexander, D., Heaviside, S., & Farris, E. (1998, December). *Status of education reform in public elementary and secondary schools: Teachers' perspectives*. U.S. DOE, OERI. NECS 1999-045. Retrieved January 29, 2002, from http://nces.ed.gov/pubs99/1999045.pdf

Barrett, H. (2001). *Using Adobe Acrobat as the ideal hypermedia format for Electronic Portfolio Development*. Retrieved January 29, 2002, from http://www.electronicportfolios.com/ portfolios/SITEacrobateportfolios.pdf

Barrett, H. (2000). *Electronic portfolios = multimedia development + portfolio development the electronic portfolio development process*. Retrieved July 23, 2001, from http://www.electronicportfolios.com/portfolios/EPDevProcess.html#stage3

Brown, G., & Irby, B.J. (2001). *The principal portfolio*. 2nd Ed. Thousand Oaks, CA: Corwin Press, Inc.

Campbell, D.M., Melenyzer, B.J., Nettles, D.H., & Wyman, R.M. (2000). *Portfolio and performance assessment*. Boston: Allyn & Bacon.

Campbell, D.M., Cignetti, P.M., Melenyzer, B.J., Nettles, D.H., & Wyman, R.M. (2001). *How to develop a professional portfolio*. 2nd Ed. Boston: Allyn & Bacon.

Collaborative for Technology Standards for School Administrators. (2001). *Technology standards for school administrators*. Retrieved January 29, 2002, from http://www.ncrtec.org/pd/tssa

Darling-Hammond, L. (Ed). (1992, September). *Model standards for beginning teaching licensing and development: A resource for state dialogue*. Washington, DC: Interstate New Teacher Assessment and Support Consortium, Council of Chief State School Officers. Retrieved January 29, 2002, from http://www.ccsso.org/intascst.html

Grant, G. E., & Huebner, T. A. (1998). The portfolio question: The power of self-directed inquiry. In Lyons, N. (Ed.), *With portfolio in hand: Validating the new teacher professionalism* (pp. 156-71). New York: Teachers College Press.

Halaydna, T. M. (1997). Writing test items to evaluate higher order thinking. Boston: Allyn & Bacon.

International Society for Technology in Education. (2000a). *Profiles for technology literate teachers: Professional preparation profile for teachers.* Retrieved January 29, http://cnets.iste.org/propro.html

International Society for Technology in Education. (2000b). *Technology standards and performance indicators for teachers.* Retrieved January 29, 2002, from http://cnets.iste.org/teachstandintro.html

International Society for Technology in Education. (2000c). *ISTE national educational technology standards (NETS•T) and performance indicators: Educational technology foundations for all teachers.* Retrieved January 29, 2002, from http://cnets.iste.org/teachstand.html

Interstate School Leaders Licensure Consortium. (1996). *Standards for school leaders.* Washington, DC: Council of Chief State School Officers. Retrieved January 29, 2002, from http://www.ccsso.org/isllc1.html

Knowles, M. S., Holton, E. F., & Swanson, R. A. (2001). *The adult learner: The definitive classic in adult education and human resource development.* 5th Ed. Woburn, MA: Butterworth-Heinemann.

Lieberman, D.A., & Rueter, J. (1997). The electronically augmented teaching portfolio. In P. Seldin (Ed.), *The teaching portfolio: A practical guide to improved performance and promotion/tenure decisions.* 2nd Ed. (pp. 47 - 57). Bolton, MA: Anker Publishing.

Lyons, N. (1998). Portfolios and their consequences: Developing as a reflective practitioner. In Lyons, N. (Ed.), *With portfolio in hand: Validating the new teacher professionalism* (pp. 23-37). New York: Teachers College Press.

Merriam-Webster Incorporated. (2002). Merriam-Webster's Collegiate Dictionary. Retrieved January 29, 2002, from http://merriamwebster.com/cgi-bin/dictionary

National Board for Professional Teaching Standards. (2001a). *National Board for Professional Teaching Standards: What teachers should know and be able to do.* Retrieved January 29, 2002, from http://www.nbpts.org/standards/five_core.html

National Board for Professional Teaching Standards. (2001b). *NBPTS 2001-2002 candidate resource center.* Retrieved January 29, 2002, from http://www.nbpts.org/candidates/2001_02/portfolio/index.html

National Commission on Excellence in Education. (1983). *A nation at risk.* Washington, D.C.: U.S. Government Printing Office.

National Commission on Teaching & America's Future. (1996, September). *What matters most: Teaching for America's future.* New York: Author.

National Council for the Accreditation of Teacher Education. (2001a). *Professional standards for the accreditation of schools, colleges, and departments of education.* Washington, D.C.: Author.

National Council for the Accreditation of Teacher Education. (2001b). *A Decade of Growth 1991–2001.* Retrieved January 29, 2002, from http://www.ncate.org/newsbrfs/dec_report.htm

Shackelford, R. L. (1997, May/June). Student portfolios: A process/product learning and assessment strategy. *The Technology Teacher, 55* (8), 31-36.

Shulman, L. (1998). Teacher portfolios: A theoretical activity. In Lyons, N. (Ed.), *With portfolio in hand: Validating the new teacher professionalism* (pp. 23-37). New York: Teachers College Press.

U.S. Department of Education. (2000). *Building bridges: The mission & principles of professional development.* Retrieved January 29, 2002, from http://www.ed.gov/G2K/bridge.html

Williams, R., & Tollett, Williams, J. (2000). *The Non-designers Web Book: An easy guide to creating, designing, and posting your own website.* 2nd Ed. Berkeley, California: Peachpit Press.

Wolf, K. (1996, March). Developing an Effective Teaching Portfolio. *Educational Leadership, 53* (6) p 34-37.

Wolf, K., & Deitz, M. (1998, Winter). Teaching portfolios: Purposes and possibilities. *Teacher Education Quarterly, 25* (1), 9 - 22.

# index